STREAMS OF MERCY

TRUTH FOR LIFE®

THE BIBLE-TEACHING MINISTRY OF **ALISTAIR BEGG**

The mission of Truth For Life is to teach the Bible with clarity and relevance so that unbelievers will be converted, believers will be established, and local churches will be strengthened.

Daily Program

Each day, Truth For Life distributes the Bible teaching of Alistair Begg across the U.S. and in several locations outside of the U.S. on over 1,800 radio outlets. To find a radio station near you, visit **truthforlife.org/stationfinder**.

Free Teaching

The daily program, and Truth For Life's entire teaching archive of over 2,000 Bible-teaching messages, can be accessed for free online and through Truth For Life's full-feature mobile app. Download the free mobile app at **truthforlife.org/app** and listen free online at **truthforlife.org**.

At-Cost Resources

Books and full-length teaching from Alistair Begg on CD, DVD, and MP3CD are available for purchase at cost, with no markup. Visit **truthforlife.org/store**.

Where to Begin?

If you're new to Truth For Life and would like to know where to begin listening and learning, find starting point suggestions at **truthforlife.org/firststep**. For a full list of ways to connect with Truth For Life, visit **truthforlife.org/subscribe**.

Contact Truth For Life

P.O. Box 398000 Cleveland, Ohio 44139
phone 1 (888) 588-7884   **email** letters@truthforlife.org
 /truthforlife @truthforlife truthforlife.org

STREAMS OF MERCY

PRAYERS OF
CONFESSION
AND
CELEBRATION

BARBARA R. DUGUID

EDITED BY IAIN M. DUGUID

P&R
PUBLISHING
P.O. BOX 817 • PHILLIPSBURG • NEW JERSEY 08865-0817

Printed in the United States of America

Library of Congress Cataloging-in-Publication Data

Names: Duguid, Barbara R., author. | Duguid, Iain M., editor.
Title: Streams of mercy : prayers of confession and celebration / Barbara R. Duguid, Iain M. Duguid.
Description: Phillipsburg : P&R Publishing, 2018. | Includes index.
Identifiers: LCCN 2017055634| ISBN 9781629953427 (pbk.) | ISBN 9781629953434 (epub) | ISBN 9781629953441 (mobi)
Subjects: LCSH: Prayers.
Classification: LCC BV245 .D84 2018 | DDC 203/.8--dc23
LC record available at https://lccn.loc.gov/2017055634

To my son Jamie,
who floods my life with friendship, mercy, kindness, and love,
and who teaches me many wonderful things.

Come, thou Fount of every blessing,
Tune my heart to sing thy grace;
Streams of mercy, never ceasing,
Call for songs of loudest praise.
Teach me some melodious sonnet,
Sung by flaming tongues above.
Praise the mount, I'm fixed upon it,
Mount of thy redeeming love.
—ROBERT ROBINSON, 1759

CONTENTS

CONTENTS

CONTENTS

PREFACE

As I wrote in my foreword to *Prone to Wander,* "Confession is good for the soul."[*] That remains true for all of us. We are deeply sinful creatures, even after we have been redeemed by God. Our thoughts, our words, and our deeds are often shaped by our idolatries far more than they are by the gospel. We think, say, and do things that we ought not to think, say, and do. And often we don't think, say, and do the things we should. Indeed, even when we are doing the very best things—reading our Bibles, praying, serving our families and our churches—our motives are shaded by all kinds of self-interest and self-promotion. In his letter "Man in his Fallen Estate," John Newton details at length the sad state of our fallen condition, not merely before our conversion but after it, and not merely in the worst of people but in the very best.[†]

That is why the Bible tells us not to pretend that we are practically perfect, but instead to confess our sins, remembering that God is faithful and just and will forgive all our sins for the sake of Jesus Christ (see 1 John 1:8–9). Our firm hope of salvation rests not on our own progress toward holiness, which is always far less than it should be, but rather on Christ's death, which atoned for every one of our sins, and on his perfect righteousness, which now clothes us like a spotless festival garment (see Zech. 3).

Historic church liturgies therefore always featured corporate confession as a central element.[‡] Yet we live in a therapeutic culture that is uncomfortable with acknowledging and owning the fact that we ourselves are unclean, as is the community around us

---

[*] Barbara R. Duguid and Wayne Duguid Houk, *Prone to Wander: Prayers of Confession and Celebration* (Phillipsburg, NJ: P&R, 2014), 11.

[†] See "Man in His Fallen Estate (1)," in *Select Letters of John Newton* (repr., Edinburgh: Banner of Truth, 2011) 117–23.

[‡] See Bryan Chapell, *Christ-Centered Worship* (Grand Rapids: Baker, 2009) 89.

(see Isa. 6). Even in our private prayers, we have often neglected the teaching of Jesus' model prayer, "Forgive us our debts, as we also have forgiven our debtors" (Matt. 6:12), or we repeat those words verbatim as a mindless slogan, never reflecting on what our own specific personal debts might be.

It is for these reasons that Barb and our son Wayne began writing corporate prayers of confession for each Sunday's service at Christ Presbyterian Church in Grove City, Pennsylvania—a practice that Barb has continued more recently at Christ Presbyterian Church in Philadelphia. These prayers are built around the theme of the Scripture passage for each week's sermon, and they seek to expose the specifics of our own struggles with sin. In that way, we are regularly pointed back to the good news of the gospel and we may hear afresh the affirmation of our own forgiveness through God's grace to us in Jesus Christ.

The structure of these confessions is straightforward. We begin with a scriptural call to confession, which roots and grounds our confession in God's Word. We want to be clear that the actions and attitudes we are calling people to confess are genuinely sinful, not simply breaches in the traditions and rules of men (see Mark 7:5–13). The Bible is to be our sole rule of faith and practice, and the scriptural call to confession underlines that reality. In most cases, the prayers are explicitly Trinitarian, confessing our many failings to the Father, giving thanks to the Son for his death on the cross as well as for his perfect (and specific) obedience in our place, which is credited to us by faith, and asking the Holy Spirit to strengthen us to pursue lives of new obedience.

The purpose of confessing our sins is always to remind us of what a great Savior we have. We confess that "there is no health in us" in order that our hearts may be drawn afresh to the Great Physician of our souls, who has provided for our desperate need for cleansing in the gospel. For that reason, we always follow each prayer of confession with a scriptural assurance of pardon: God's authoritative declaration that each and every one of the sins of his people is forgiven in Jesus Christ. This is our only hope in life and death. These assurances, too, we have endeavored to make specific, providing gospel encouragement that is tailored to our particular failings and that points us afresh to the new life that is ours in Christ.

These prayers may be used as an aid in private devotions or as a help to those who lead God's people in worship. We have supplied indexes of themes, of Scriptures cited, and of the sermon passages that originally gave us the focus for these particular prayers when we shared them with our congregations. There is also an index of hymns and songs, which lists some of the music that went with the prayers in their original worship context, as well as allusions to hymns and songs within the prayers themselves. We give permission for people to adapt and adopt this material for such use in corporate worship services as will bless the church.

Our debt to others in this compilation is not hard to see. Arthur Bennett's *The Valley of Vision** was a model for us, in both its scope and its rich and evocative language of devotion. We are also indebted to the team at P&R for many hours of hard work in helping us bring this material to its final form.

It is our prayer that God will continue to use these prayers in the lives of many people, so that we may once again rediscover that, as Martin Luther put it in the first of his ninety-five theses, "the entire Christian life is to be one of repentance."

IAIN M. DUGUID

---

* Arthur G. Bennett, *The Valley of Vision: A Collection of Puritan Prayers and Devotions* (Edinburgh: Banner of Truth, 1975).

THE HEART

✤ CALL TO CONFESSION: GENESIS 6:5–6;
   JOEL 2:12–14

The LORD saw that the wickedness of man was great in the earth, and that every intention of the thoughts of his heart was only evil continually. And the LORD regretted that he had made man on the earth, and it grieved him to his heart.

"Yet even now," declares the LORD,
   "return to me with all your heart,
with fasting, with weeping, and with mourning;
   and rend your hearts and not your garments."
Return to the LORD your God,
   for he is gracious and merciful,
slow to anger, and abounding in steadfast love;
   and he relents over disaster.
Who knows whether he will not turn and relent,
   and leave a blessing behind him,
a grain offering and a drink offering
   for the LORD your God?

✤ PRAYER OF CONFESSION

Mighty God,
   Your Word penetrates our hearts and exposes the truth about our thoughts and intentions. It uncovers our self-confidence and self-centeredness, as well as the secret sins that we hide so successfully from one another. The truth is that we cherish and love many evil thoughts in our hearts, even when outwardly we pretend to be full of spiritual desires. We harbor hatred and anger for those around us, along with jealousy and pride. We judge and condemn others in our hearts, or we envy them and lust after them. Even our good deeds are deeply stained by wrong motives. We often wait to serve others until people are watching us, so that we may be admired and glorified. We speak your

truth impatiently and harshly in order to prove ourselves. Father, forgive us not just for our sinful actions but for our corrupt and perverse hearts.

Jesus, thank you that you came to deliver us from our sinful self-centeredness. Your heart was always perfectly aligned with the Father's Word. Your thoughts as well as your actions were always pure and undefiled, filled with love for those around you and compassion for lost people. You worked hard in the Father's service, but you also rested confidently in the Father's power. Even though you are the Lord of Glory and eternally deserving of praise, you never glorified yourself. Instead, you laid aside your glory and became a humble servant, defeating the forces of Satan through your own death and winning victory in our place.

Holy Spirit, teach us not to trust in ourselves or in earthly sources of power and strength. Enable us to trust completely in Jesus, our great High Priest, who faithfully intercedes for us. Help us not to be unduly discouraged by the heavy load of guilt that so easily clings to our hearts. Instead, whenever we see clearly the sins of our hearts, enable us to fly to the Scriptural truth that in Christ the penalty of those sins has been paid for, once for all. Remind us that we are now clothed in Christ's perfect righteousness, and that therefore there can be no condemnation left for us. In Christ's name we pray, amen.

❧ ASSURANCE OF PARDON: JEREMIAH 32:39–41; ROMANS 6:17–18

"I will give them one heart and one way, that they may fear me forever, for their own good and the good of their children after them. I will make with them an everlasting covenant, that I will not turn away from doing good to them. And I will put the fear of me in their hearts, that they may not turn from me. I will rejoice in doing them good, and I will plant them in this land in faithfulness, with all my heart and all my soul."

But thanks be to God, that you who were once slaves of sin have become obedient from the heart to the standard of teaching to which you were committed, and, having been set free from sin, have become slaves of righteousness.

✤ HYMNS

"God, Be Merciful to Me"
"Nothing That My Hands Can Do"

NO OTHER GODS (COMMANDMENT 1)

✤ CALL TO CONFESSION: EXODUS 20:1–3; DEUTERONOMY 6:4–9

And God spoke all these words, saying,

"I am the LORD your God, who brought you out of the land of Egypt, out of the house of slavery.

You shall have no other gods before me."

"Hear, O Israel: The LORD our God, the LORD is one. You shall love the LORD your God with all your heart and with all your soul and with all your might. And these words that I command you today shall be on your heart. You shall teach them diligently to your children, and shall talk of them when you sit in your house, and when you walk by the way, and when you lie down, and when you rise. You shall bind them as a sign on your hand, and they shall be as frontlets between your eyes. You shall write them on the doorposts of your house and on your gates."

✤ PRAYER OF CONFESSION

Eternal Father,

Your kindness and love are beyond all thought, far exceeding our wildest dreams. But, Lord, we are not like you. Our lips may confess our devotion to you, but our hearts are slow to follow our words, and we are reluctant to obey you with our lives. We confess to you our adulterous and idolatrous hearts. We cherish many things far more than we love you, and we spend hours each day worshiping at the feet of other gods. Instead of treasuring you and your Word, we lavish the best of our time on our false gods, hoping that they will bless us and reward us for our efforts. Meanwhile, we are content to give you the leftovers of our attention. O God, have mercy on us and forgive us for our persistent blindness and false worship.

Holy Spirit, give us grace to hate and grieve the many moments we have spent lost in worship before our other lovers. We have turned your good gifts into false gods and have given ourselves to them. Even though they use and abuse us, still we run after them and sell our souls to them. Please work in us continual repentance, turning our wandering hearts back to our perfect Savior. Teach us to love your Word, which reminds us that he has loved us and given himself for us; he traded all of the glory of heaven in order to live with us and be obedient for us.

Make Christ beautiful to us. Satisfy our minds with true knowledge of him, and set our hearts on fire with profound love for him. Let us love him with every part of ourselves: with emotions that delight in him and long for him; with minds that are full of thoughts of him and bodies that are eager to serve him. Draw us back to the cross, where his love was poured out for the salvation of our souls. Remind us that even death will never part us from you, but can only be the bright and joyful completion of your eternal story of love and redemption. In Jesus' beautiful name we pray, amen.

✤ ASSURANCE OF PARDON: 1 JOHN 3:1; 4:9–10

See what kind of love the Father has given to us, that we should be called children of God; and so we are.

In this the love of God was made manifest among us, that God sent his only Son into the world, so that we might live through him. In this is love, not that we have loved God but that he loved us and sent his Son to be the propitiation for our sins.

✤ HYMNS

"Here Is Love Vast as the Ocean"
"My Jesus, I Love Thee"

NO IDOLS
(COMMANDMENT 2)

✦ CALL TO CONFESSION: EXODUS 20:4–6;
   ROMANS 1:22–25

"You shall not make for yourself a carved image, or any likeness of anything that is in heaven above, or that is in the earth beneath, or that is in the water under the earth. You shall not bow down to them or serve them, for l the LORD your God am a jealous God, visiting the iniquity of the fathers on the children to the third and the fourth generation of those who hate me, but showing steadfast love to thousands of those who love me and keep my commandments."

Claiming to be wise, they became fools, and exchanged the glory of the immortal God for images resembling mortal man and birds and animals and creeping things.

Therefore God gave them up in the lusts of their hearts to impurity, to the dishonoring of their bodies among themselves, because they exchanged the truth about God for a lie and worshiped and served the creature rather than the Creator, who is blessed forever! Amen.

✦ PRAYER OF CONFESSION

Loving heavenly Father,

You have created us to worship you alone. Fashioned by your hand and kept alive each moment by your will and your decree, we depend on you for each breath that we take. You have dealt kindly and patiently with us, and we should worship you alone, with joy and gratitude, every moment of every day. Your Word should delight us and your law should motivate us to obedience, all day every day. Yet, Lord, we are great sinners who wander and run from you often. We regularly exchange your truth for lies, because we don't want to worship and obey you. Rather, we want to be our own gods. Many times each day we turn from you toward the idols that enchant us, bowing before them and hoping that they will make peace for us. We desire sinful things and sell our souls to get them. We treasure your gifts instead of treasuring you, feeling that we can't live without the good things you have given us. Father, forgive us; have mercy on us, for we are weak and guilty of worshiping many false gods.

Thank you for Jesus, who paid the price for all our sin and who worshiped you alone throughout his earthly life. When tempted to bow before Satan and to pursue the glittering jewels of fame, power, and wealth, he stood firm and prized you and obedience to you above all things. Knowing that we would desperately need his righteousness to cover our shame, he persevered, and now you have given us all his goodness. Father, thank you that you have given us a mighty Redeemer, and that you have left your Holy Spirit within us until your work on earth is done.

Holy Spirit, show us our idolatry and grant us sweet conviction and joyful repentance. Make Christ more beautiful to us than all other things, and help us to desire him above the trinkets and positions of power that we crave. Grant us a growing hope and faith in Christ alone, until the day when we bow before our victorious King, rescued by his strong arm and dressed in his righteousness alone. In his mighty name we pray, amen.

✤ ASSURANCE OF PARDON: EZEKIEL 37:23, 26

"They shall not defile themselves anymore with their idols and their detestable things, or with any of their transgressions. But I will save them from all the backslidings in which they have sinned, and will cleanse them; and they shall be my people, and I will be their God.

. . . I will make a covenant of peace with them. It shall be an everlasting covenant with them. And I will set them in their land and multiply them, and will set my sanctuary in their midst forevermore."

✤ HYMNS

"Jesus, Be My All (How Sad Our State)"
"There Is a Redeemer"

GOD'S NAME (COMMANDMENT 3)

✤ CALL TO CONFESSION: EXODUS 20:7; GENESIS 11:4; ISAIAH 42:8

"You shall not take the name of the Lord your God in vain, for the Lord will not hold him guiltless who takes his name in vain."

Then they said, "Come, let us build ourselves a city and a tower with its top in the heavens, and let us make a name for ourselves, lest we be dispersed over the face of the whole earth."

"I am the Lord; that is my name;
 my glory I give to no other,
 nor my praise to carved idols."

✤ PRAYER OF CONFESSION

Mighty and majestic God,

We come to you as deeply self-centered people. You have been so much better to us than we deserve, faithfully fulfilling your commitment to give us good things in Christ, and you deserve all glory and honor to be given to your name. Yet we want the glory to accrue to our names instead. We quickly forget all the wonderful gifts that you have given us, and we act as if our achievements were the result of our own efforts while our failures belonged to someone else. Instead of remembering our utter dependence upon you and running to you daily as our shield of refuge, we prefer to give ourselves over to our idols because we love our sins and it seems too costly to fight against them. We are overconfident in our own strength, and we doubt your goodness and power many times each day. Father, forgive us.

Jesus, thank you for your humble obedience on our behalf. You worshiped your Father and glorified his name daily, with unwavering faith and unshakeable hope in his goodness. Cherishing the Father's unchangeable character, you submitted to his perfect wisdom and trusted him completely in all of the circumstances of your life, even when it was most painful. You took refuge in him often in your times of need and never turned toward false gods or sought your own comfort and glory. Now your name encourages us to hope in the midst of continuing weakness, confident that you will continue to advocate our cause as our heavenly high priest. We have no other name in which to trust, nor do we need one.

Holy Spirit, we need your power at work in us to stir up our weak faith. Help us to know and worship our God as he truly is: the unchangeable, sovereign, wise King who has sworn by himself to save us in spite of our foolishness. Cause us to know the certainty of God's great love for us, until we are transformed into people who love him deeply and are able to run the race of obedience humbly, with strong confidence and joyful hope in Christ. Open our lips to join the heavenly worship service as we look forward to the return of our heavenly King. Amen.

✤ ASSURANCE OF PARDON: ACTS 4:11–12; ROMANS 10:9–10, 12–13

"This Jesus is the stone that was rejected by you, the builders, which has become the cornerstone. And there is salvation in no one else, for there is no other name under heaven given among men by which we must be saved."

If you confess with your mouth that Jesus is Lord and believe in your heart that God raised him from the dead, you will be saved. For with the heart one believes and is justified, and with the mouth one confesses and is saved. . . . For there is no distinction between Jew and Greek; for the same Lord is Lord of all, bestowing his riches on all who call on him. For "everyone who calls on the name of the Lord will be saved."

✤ HYMNS

"Depth of Mercy"
"O for a Thousand Tongues"

SABBATH (COMMANDMENT 4)

✤ CALL TO CONFESSION: EXODUS 20:8–11; ISAIAH 58:13–14

"Remember the Sabbath day, to keep it holy. Six days you shall labor, and do all your work, but the seventh day is a Sabbath to the LORD your God. On it you shall not do any work, you, or your son, or your daughter, your male servant, or your female servant, or your livestock, or the sojourner who is within your gates. For in six days the LORD made heaven and earth, the sea, and all that is in them, and rested on the seventh day. Therefore the LORD blessed the Sabbath day and made it holy."

"If you turn back your foot from the Sabbath,
    from doing your pleasure on my holy day,
and call the Sabbath a delight
    and the holy day of the LORD honorable;
if you honor it, not going your own ways,
    or seeking your own pleasure, or talking idly;
then you shall take delight in the LORD,
    and I will make you ride on the heights of the earth;
I will feed you with the heritage of Jacob your father,
    for the mouth of the LORD has spoken."

✤ PRAYER OF CONFESSION

Creator God,

At the beginning of time you created a day of rest, a sign pointing forward to the eternal rest that we will share with you forever. You now ask your people to set aside one day in seven—to rest and to worship; to remember our deliverance from bondage to sin; to know that all our needs come from your hands. We thank you for this precious gift, yet we misuse it in so many ways. For some of us it is a day to keep rules, impress others with our piety, and parade our righteousness instead of needing yours. We dress our bodies for church while our hearts are cold, filled with pride and self-sufficiency. We display our spiritual victories for others to admire, yet we don't confess the sinfulness we struggle with moment by moment. We memorize Scripture and catechisms, we lift our hands in prayer, and we serve energetically, relying on our own goodness as though it could ever satisfy you. Father, forgive us.

For some of us, Sunday is a day like any other day: a day to catch up on work, to play and recreate with no thought of you and no desire to make worship and fellowship a priority. We foolishly believe that we can love you well on our own, without the brothers and sisters with whom you have called us to walk through life. We feel little awe and reverence for you or gratitude for all you have done. Our appetite for your Word is small, while our belief in our own understanding looms large. We are wise in our own eyes, and we fail to see the consequences of our selfish and immature behavior. Lord, have mercy on us in our weakness and sin.

Jesus, you loved your Father above all and delighted to worship and study in his house. From your childhood, you were a careful scholar, dedicating yourself to studying and teaching others. You loved to pray and withdrew often to meditate and speak with your heavenly Father. Your heart was never cold, but always warmly devoted to living in gratitude, faith, and obedience. Jesus, thank you for honoring the Sabbath for us, in your heart and with your body. You courageously faced every temptation to misuse it, standing firm because you knew we would need your goodness to stand before a holy God. Thank you, precious Savior.

Holy Spirit, correct our thinking and strengthen our souls. We are blind and deceived by our own wisdom; open our eyes and show us our hearts. Remind us of the love of Christ until our hearts are humbly drawn to hunger for God's Word preached faithfully. Help us to understand your Word and to know what you ask of us. Help us to believe that you are loving and that all your commands are good for us and are meant for our joy and growth. Holy Spirit, help us to worship wholeheartedly, and strengthen us with the body and blood of Christ at the Lord's Table. Enable us to love other believers, even when it feels uncomfortable to be in church. May all other things seem small and insignificant compared to loving and obeying you well, as we look forward to worshiping you forever, gathered with all the saints around your throne. Amen.

✤ ASSURANCE OF PARDON: MATTHEW 11:28–30

"Come to me, all who labor and are heavy laden, and I will give you rest. Take my yoke upon you, and learn from me, for I am gentle and lowly in heart, and you will find rest for your souls. For my yoke is easy, and my burden is light."

✤ HYMNS

"I'll Rest in Christ"
"I Heard the Voice of Jesus Say"
"Jesus, I am Resting, Resting"
"Loved with Everlasting Love"

HONORING PARENTS (COMMANDMENT 5)

✤ CALL TO CONFESSION: EXODUS 20:12;
MATTHEW 15:4–8

"Honor your father and your mother, that your days may be long in the land that the LORD your God is giving you."

"For God commanded, 'Honor your father and your mother,' and, 'Whoever reviles father or mother must surely die.' But you say, 'If anyone tells his father or his mother, "What you would have gained from me is given to God," he need not honor his father.' So for the sake of your tradition you have made void the word of God. You hypocrites! Well did Isaiah prophesy of you, when he said:

"'This people honors me with their lips,
but their heart is far from me.'"

✤ PRAYER OF CONFESSION

Almighty God, precious heavenly Father,
    You alone are worthy of all honor and praise, and to worship and adore you is our noblest privilege. You deserve honor, respect, and obedience from all of your creatures, for you have made them and your will alone gives them life and purpose. You are the King of Kings and Lord of Lords. Creation is full of your glory, and you have given us all things richly to enjoy. All your works praise you; all your saints bless and honor you. Let us be numbered with your holy ones who gather around your throne. Let us join them in their endless adoration, sit with them at the feet of Jesus, and grow to resemble them in godly character.
    Father, forgive us for the many ways in which we sin against your wise commands. As children, we fail to honor our parents. We are prone to give way to rebellious, arrogant, selfish, and

demanding hearts that disobey and dishonor those whom you have commanded us to respect. As parents, we often exasperate and sin against our children, making it difficult for them to keep this commandment and obscuring their ability to know and love you. Every day we must confess that we honor you with our lips while our hearts are given over to the worship of our favorite idols. Father, forgive us and have mercy on us, for we are wretched sinners. We thank you for the radiant beauty of your perfect Son, who honored you with flawless obedience and reverence. Cover us with his goodness and clothe us in his righteousness. Look upon us and see him, for the sake of his glorious name.

Holy Spirit, deliver us from the darkness of our minds, the corruption of our hearts, the temptations of the evil one, and the dangerous snares in the world that surrounds us. Show us our disrespectful thoughts toward you and toward our parents, and help us to repent. Humble us and fill us with gratitude that will melt our cold hearts and match the words of love and loyalty that cross our lips so easily. Help us to love and honor imperfect parents for your sake. Enable us to parent with wisdom, compassion, and gentleness. Make us quick repenters who confess our sin readily to one another and fly swiftly to the throne of your grace to find help in our great need. Let us celebrate every day the enormous love you have displayed toward us in sacrificing your most precious treasure, your only Son, so that we could be your children. In Jesus's name we pray, amen.

✤ ASSURANCE OF PARDON: FROM 1 PETER 2:4–7, 9–10

As you come to him, a living stone rejected by men but in the sight of God chosen and precious, you yourselves like living stones are being built up as a spiritual house, to be a holy priesthood, to offer spiritual sacrifices acceptable to God through Jesus Christ. For it stands in Scripture:

"Behold, I am laying in Zion a stone,
    a cornerstone chosen and precious,
and whoever believes in him will not be put to shame."

So the honor is for you who believe. . . .

 . . . You are a chosen race, a royal priesthood, a holy nation, a people for his own possession, that you may proclaim the excellencies of him who called you out of darkness into his marvelous light. Once you were not a people, but now you are God's people; once you had not received mercy, but now you have received mercy.

✤ HYMNS

"How Deep the Father's Love"
"Wonderful, Merciful Savior"

ANGER
(COMMANDMENT 6)

✤ CALL TO CONFESSION: EXODUS 20:13; MATTHEW 5:20–22; 10:28–31

"You shall not murder."

"For I tell you, unless your righteousness exceeds that of the scribes and Pharisees, you will never enter the kingdom of heaven.

"You have heard that it was said to those of old, 'You shall not murder; and whoever murders will be liable to judgment.' But I say to you that everyone who is angry with his brother will be liable to judgment; whoever insults his brother will be liable to the council; and whoever says, 'You fool!' will be liable to the hell of fire."

"And do not fear those who kill the body but cannot kill the soul. Rather fear him who can destroy both soul and body in hell. Are not two sparrows sold for a penny? And not one of them will fall to the ground apart from your Father. But even the hairs of your head are all numbered. Fear not, therefore; you are of more value than many sparrows."

✤ PRAYER OF CONFESSION

O Lord,

We marvel that you would take on flesh and blood in order to be crucified, killed, and buried for us. You humbled yourself and submitted to the hatred of sinful men, accepting the thorns, the whip, the nails, and the spear, to free us from sin and death forever. Although you dreaded the pain and the separation from your Father, you loved him more than life, and for the joy of having us as brothers and sisters you endured the cross of shame.

We praise you for your costly obedience, because you have paid the enormous debt of all our sin, and because we desperately need your righteousness to stand in place of our unrighteousness. Although most of us have not actually killed anyone, we confess that we have all hated, and continue to hate, others in our hearts. Our hearts rise up often to judge others, to disdain and condemn them, to dismiss them from our circle of friends, to murder the reputation of others through gossip and slander. We are capable of great unkindness toward enemies and loved ones when we feel fearful, threatened, and disrespected. Lord, forgive us for our unruly, self-centered, and murderous hearts.

Precious Savior, we cannot change our hearts. Through the power of your Spirit we ask for more grace to see the truth about ourselves. Help us to confess honestly our hatred of you and of one another. We plead for repentance; help us to die to ourselves more deeply. Make us people who breathe life into others with words of encouragement and edification, instead of hating with our hearts and killing with our lips. Holy Spirit, crucify our sinful desires and make us like Christ. Ravish our hearts with the truth of the gospel. Transform us by your powerful love so that we may truly love others and raise them up. Form us into people who endure costly relational pain for the sake of loving and forgiving our worst enemies.

Jesus, we thank you that we will not struggle with ugly, sinful hearts forever. The empty tomb calls forth our adoring wonder, for just as surely as that tomb is empty, we too will be given new life. Your return in triumphant new life proves your victory over our sin; it assures us that in the death of our sinful flesh, we too will be resurrected to lives of perfect holiness, obedience, and love. The resurrection fills us with hope and joy that the battle has been won and that you will walk with us faithfully until you welcome us into heaven to live with you forever. Amen! Come, Lord Jesus; come quickly!

✤ ASSURANCE OF PARDON: JOHN 11:25–26; 5:24–26

Jesus said to her, "I am the resurrection and the life. Whoever believes in me, though he die, yet shall he live, and everyone who lives and believes in me shall never die. Do you believe this?"

"Truly, truly, I say to you, whoever hears my word and believes him who sent me has eternal life. He does not come into judgment, but has passed from death to life.

"Truly, truly, I say to you, an hour is coming, and is now here, when the dead will hear the voice of the Son of God, and those who hear will live. For as the Father has life in himself, so he has granted the Son also to have life in himself."

✤ HYMNS

"Poor Sinner Dejected with Fear"
"Thine Be the Glory"

LUST
(COMMANDMENT 7)

✤ **CALL TO CONFESSION: EXODUS 20:14; 19:5–6; EZEKIEL 16:15; MATTHEW 5:27–29**

"You shall not commit adultery."

✤✤✤

"Now therefore, if you will indeed obey my voice and keep my covenant, you shall be my treasured possession among all peoples, for all the earth is mine; and you shall be to me a kingdom of priests and a holy nation."

✤✤✤

"But you trusted in your beauty and played the whore because of your renown and lavished your whorings on any passerby; your beauty became his."

✤✤✤

[Jesus said] "You have heard that it was said, 'You shall not commit adultery.' But I say to you that everyone who looks at a woman with lustful intent has already committed adultery with her in his heart. If your right eye causes you to sin, tear it out and throw it away. For it is better that you lose one of your members than that your whole body be thrown into hell."

✤ **PRAYER OF CONFESSION**

Heavenly Father,

We confess before you the many ways in which we have abused our sexuality. Lord, instead of delighting in sex as a glorious gift of deep intimacy within marriage, we have twisted it in many ways. We have used sex to pursue false intimacy in serial relationships, either in actuality or in our minds. We have sold our purity to purchase love and acceptance, or to fill the emptiness and loneliness in our hearts. Our sexuality has been squandered in service of our idols, instead of being honored and guarded as you intended. Some of us have been deeply affected by sexual abuse, which leaves profound scars on this area of our lives. Others are proud of our pretended purity, but our hearts are as defiled as everyone else's. Instead of being a reflection of your passionate, jealous, and unique commitment to your people, our sexuality is a cesspool of divided loyalties and self-serving acts. What you made good, we have defiled.

Lord, when the shame of our broken sexuality threatens to overwhelm us, help us to flee to the cross. We praise you for Jesus, your perfect Son—even though he was endowed with normal sexual desires, he resisted sexual temptation perfectly, knowing that we would need his obedience to cover us and enable us to stand joyfully before you. His righteousness is sufficient for us in this area as well, whether our failures are physical or mental, heterosexual or same-sex oriented, related to pornography or romantic fantasy literature.

Holy Spirit, for the sake of your holy name, cleanse our hearts from our idols. Enable us to guard our minds and our eyes in the midst of a sex-saturated culture. Give us grace within our marriages to serve and enjoy each other through our sexuality as a way of developing and experiencing deep union together. Teach us to encourage one another in our struggles and failures and to comfort those who fall with the good news of the gospel. Help our churches to support those who are not married with a network of intimate relationships, in which they are profoundly known, loved, and cherished. Amen.

❖ ASSURANCE OF PARDON: 1 CORINTHIANS 6:9–11; 2 CORINTHIANS 5:17

Do you not know that the unrighteous will not inherit the kingdom of God? Do not be deceived: neither the sexually immoral, nor idolaters, nor adulterers, nor men who practice homosexuality, nor thieves, nor the greedy, nor drunkards, nor revilers, nor swindlers will inherit the kingdom of God. And such were some of you. But you were washed, you were sanctified, you were justified in the name of the Lord Jesus Christ and by the Spirit of our God.

Therefore, if anyone is in Christ, he is a new creation. The old has passed away; behold, the new has come.

❖ HYMNS

"Come, Thou Fount of Every Blessing"
"God, Be Merciful to Me"

STEALING
(COMMANDMENT 8)

✤ CALL TO CONFESSION: EXODUS 20:15;
PROVERBS 30:8–9; MATTHEW 6:19–21

"You shall not steal."

✤✤✤

Give me neither poverty nor riches;
    feed me with the food that is needful for me,
lest I be full and deny you
    and say, "Who is the LORD?"
or lest I be poor and steal
    and profane the name of my God.

✤✤✤

"Do not lay up for yourselves treasures on earth, where moth and rust destroy and where thieves break in and steal, but lay up for yourselves treasures in heaven, where neither moth nor rust destroys and where thieves do not break in and steal. For where your treasure is, there your heart will be also."

✤ PRAYER OF CONFESSION

Blessed Lord Jesus,

Help us to give up every precious lust on which we squander our longings. We have treasured many objects above our Savior and have carefully nurtured storehouses of idols that demand our worship. Forgive us for accumulating riches and finding our salvation, joy, and identity in them. When you give us good gifts, we are prone to love them too much and to cling to them, instead of thanking you for them and clinging to you. We rejoice too much in the wealth you send, and we despair too much when you take it away. Father, forgive us.

Teach us to delight instead in all the spiritual riches you have lavished on us so extravagantly in Christ: the wealth of his righteousness given to us; the riches of his grace and kindness poured out on us; the generous inheritance he has earned for us by his perfect obedience and death. Remind us often of who we are in Christ, as we walk through a world of temptation that dazzles and beckons us, and as we wrestle with sinful hearts full of desires and over-desires. Draw our hearts and minds to the cross daily so we will understand how we have been cherished, and captivate our minds and souls with this great love.

Gracious Redeemer, we have neglected you often and cruci-fied you afresh by our repeated sin. Yet you set your love on us before the creation of the world and treasured us as the reward of all your obedience and suffering. Melt our hearts daily with gratitude for such a love. We thank you for your patience that has borne with us so long, and for the grace that makes us willing to be yours. We ask for more grace for obedience, so that we desire what you desire and do what you want us to do. Unite us to yourself with inseparable bonds, so that nothing may ever draw us back from you. Keep us safe until that day when we will see what no eye has seen, will hear what no ear has heard, and will know what no human mind has ever conceived—all the glorious things you have prepared for us in heaven. Thank you, Lord Jesus! Amen.

❖ ASSURANCE OF PARDON: MARK 10:29–30; 2 CORINTHIANS 8:9

Jesus said, "Truly, I say to you, there is no one who has left house or brothers or sisters or mother or father or children or lands, for my sake and for the gospel, who will not receive a hundredfold now in this time, houses and brothers and sisters and mothers and children and lands, with persecutions, and in the age to come eternal life."

❖❖❖

For you know the grace of our Lord Jesus Christ, that though he was rich, yet for your sake he became poor, so that you by his poverty might become rich.

❖ HYMNS

"How High and How Wide"
"When I Survey the Wondrous Cross"

FALSE WITNESS (COMMANDMENT 9)

✤ CALL TO CONFESSION: EXODUS 20:16; JAMES 3:5–6, 9–10

"You shall not bear false witness against your neighbor."

The tongue is a small member, yet it boasts of great things.

How great a forest is set ablaze by such a small fire! And the tongue is a fire, a world of unrighteousness. The tongue is set among our members, staining the whole body, setting on fire the entire course of life, and set on fire by hell. . . . With it we bless our Lord and Father, and with it we curse people who are made in the likeness of God. From the same mouth come blessing and cursing. My brothers, these things ought not to be so.

✤ PRAYER OF CONFESSION

Giver of all graces,

You are full of grace and truth, and all your mercies end in our delight. Since the dawn of time, when Satan first tempted with a lie and mankind readily chose to believe it, we have been people full of blindness and deception. In the garden, you made a promise that your goodness, kindness, and love would triumph over our rebellion, and you have kept that promise. You have never lied to us, and you have been faithful to your Word, though we have been unfaithful deceivers. Father, thank you for your grace, mercy, and truth.

We confess that truth does not reign in our innermost hearts. We are easily deceived by our own desires, and we are often sinful deceivers of others. We use our tongues to sing your praises one moment, and the next we use them to lie to ourselves, to you, and to those around us. We bear false witness against others in order to get our way, to ensure that our will is done, to make ourselves look good, to escape punishment, and for many other reasons. In our fallen sinfulness, it is easy for us to distort truth and call it honesty, and to exaggerate facts and believe our own lies. Father, forgive us for the depth and darkness of our selfish sin. Thank you for your Son, who is our way, our truth, and our life. His perfect honesty has become ours through his life and death, and now the powerful truth about him rescues us and changes us for all eternity.

Spirit of Truth, illuminate us and transform us, we pray. Convict us of our specific sins and help us to repent, for we cannot do this without your help. May the pure truth of our Father's unconditional love for liars like us humble us deeply. Let the truth of his joyful determination to save us exalt our hearts and fill us with a gleeful gratitude that lays hold of our hearts and tongues, filling them with thanksgiving and praise. We thank you that you are our advocate, our helper, and our closest friend, and that you will never leave us. Grow us in truth until the day we stand before our precious Savior and become like him forever. In his name we pray, amen.

✤ ASSURANCE OF PARDON: PSALM 145:18; JOHN 14:6, 15–18

The LORD is near to all who call on him,
to all who call on him in truth.

Jesus said to him, "I am the way, and the truth, and the life. No one comes to the Father except through me. . . ."

"If you love me, you will keep my commandments. And I will ask the Father, and he will give you another Helper, to be with you forever, even the Spirit of truth, whom the world cannot receive, because it neither sees him nor knows him. You know him, for he dwells with you and will be in you.

"I will not leave you as orphans; I will come to you."

✤ HYMNS

"Jesus, Lover of My Soul"
"Jesus! What a Friend for Sinners!"

COVETING
(COMMANDMENT 10)

❖ CALL TO CONFESSION: EXODUS 20:17;
   1 TIMOTHY 6:6–9

"You shall not covet your neighbor's house; you shall not covet your neighbor's wife, or his male servant, or his female servant, or his ox, or his donkey, or anything that is your neighbor's."

But godliness with contentment is great gain, for we brought nothing into the world, and we cannot take anything out of the world. But if we have food and clothing, with these we will be content. But those who desire to be rich fall into temptation, into a snare, into many senseless and harmful desires that plunge people into ruin and destruction.

❖ PRAYER OF CONFESSION

Generous Father,

Every good thing comes from you. You bless us each day with gifts we have not earned—such as life and breath; senses with which to enjoy this world you made for us; bodies that feel, see, smell, and touch. We have not earned these good things. In fact, we were born as rebels against you, and we use the bodies, minds, and senses you have made to sin against you daily by craving what we do not have. With our eyes, we look at others and covet what you have given to them. With our hearts, we grumble and fantasize about how to get them.

We covet the honor, power, wealth, beauty, and success we don't have, and we shake our tiny fists in your face when you withhold what we want so badly. We want better grades, more money, greater health, success at all we do. . . . The list is nearly endless, and we devote a great deal of emotional energy to yearning for what we want while despising what we do have. How easily our desires lead to fights and conflicts among us! We live in a world that is wholly governed by your perfect and sovereign will, yet we quickly grumble against you and despise others. We are weak and full of selfishness, Father—forgive us.

Holy Spirit, let us see that our sin of coveting what our neighbors have is actually a rebellion against you and a rejection of your loving provision for us. Open our eyes to the emotions and beliefs that deceive us and make us miserable with ourselves and others. Help us to see the ugly thoughts and words that flow from our jealousy, and help us to confess this sin, to repent, and to ask for forgiveness. When we see our sin and our guilt overwhelms us, lift our eyes upward from this world and show us afresh the goodness of Christ in our place: his patience and contentment with his low position and difficult calling. He never grumbled about what he didn't have or lusted after the wealth and position of others. He didn't abuse his power to get his way or accumulate things. When hungry and tempted to turn stones into bread, he was willing and able to wait for your provision at the right time. He didn't lust for power or glory, though he deserved those very things. Even when he was filled with dread before he died and you declined his request for the cup to pass from him, he did not argue or disobey, but submitted to your will and provision. Now his perfect contentment is ours. O God, fill us with a gratitude that is radically transforming and makes us willing and able to give up everything this world can offer in order to love and follow Christ. Remind us often of the great inheritance you have prepared for us; help us to wait well and to thank you humbly for every small mercy you give us each day. Amen.

❖ ASSURANCE OF PARDON: EPHESIANS 3:14–21

For this reason I bow my knees before the Father, from whom every family in heaven and on earth is named, that according to the riches of his glory he may grant you to be strengthened with power through his Spirit in your inner being, so that Christ may dwell in your hearts through faith—that you, being rooted and grounded in love, may have strength to comprehend with all the saints what is the breadth and length and height and depth, and to know the love of Christ that surpasses knowledge, that you may be filled with all the fullness of God.

Now to him who is able to do far more abundantly than all that we ask or think, according to the power at work within us, to him be glory in the church and in Christ Jesus throughout all generations, forever and ever. Amen.

✤ HYMNS

"Carried to the Table"
"Come Ye Sinners"
"The Lord's My Shepherd"

GOD'S GLORY

✢ CALL TO CONFESSION: EXODUS 33:18–23

Moses said, "Please show me your glory." And he said, "I will make
all my goodness pass before you and will proclaim before you
my name 'The LORD.' And I will be gracious to whom I will be
gracious, and will show mercy on whom I will show mercy. But,"
he said, "you cannot see my face, for man shall not see me and
live." And the LORD said, "Behold, there is a place by me where
you shall stand on the rock, and while my glory passes by I will
put you in a cleft of the rock, and I will cover you with my hand
until I have passed by. Then I will take away my hand, and you
shall see my back, but my face shall not be seen."

✢ PRAYER OF CONFESSION

Mighty God and loving heavenly Father,

You are our glorious Creator who made all things from nothing. In the beginning, you fashioned the sun, moon, and stars,
and you divided light from darkness. You gave mankind the
glory of your image, crowning us with honor and blessing. You
took great delight in your creation, gracing your image bearers
with the light of your presence as you walked with Adam in the
garden each day. But Adam fell, exchanging the glorious light
of your love for the darkness of sin and rebellion. We confess
that we were in Adam as he sinned, and we are just like Adam
as we continue to make that same choice each day. Though we
know you, we are still lovers of darkness who drift toward sin
whenever you leave us to ourselves. Even your majestic glory
can barely compete with the dazzling trinkets of this world that
captivate us. Father, forgive us.

Lord, we thank you that our sin and darkness can never
overwhelm the shining brightness of your glory and love. Though
we are drawn to disobedience in many ways, considering many
things more beautiful than you, you sent your Son to shine the
radiant light of your love on vile sinners like us. We thank you
for Jesus. Though he is the Light of the World, full of glory and

grace, he volunteered to enter our darkness and live in our flesh and blood to destroy the power of sin over us. He lived his life in shining obedience so that he could give his goodness to us as a free gift. He chose to be slain by the darkness in order to pay our debt, and we are undone by his sacrifice.

Holy Spirit, draw our hearts from darkness to light. Show us the glory of our Redeemer; cause us to revel in his love and to bask in the joy of his great pleasure in us. Enable us to hate the darkness of our sin and to flee to the brightness of his love, which welcomes us as treasured brothers and sisters who are reclothed in the brightness of his obedience. In our weakness we cannot come to you, but we ask that you would come to us over and over again. Refresh us with truth and draw us once again from the darkness we prefer to the light we so desperately need. As you did Moses, give us a strong desire to see your glory in our world and in our lives every day. Dazzle us with your beauty and goodness until our idols are revealed in all their foolishness. Help us to live not for our own glory, but for the glory of the one who gave himself to redeem us. Prepare us for the day when we will fall at Jesus' feet and will live in the bright light of his glory in our heavenly home forever. In the beautiful name of our Savior we pray, amen.

✤ ASSURANCE OF PARDON: JOHN 1:1–4, 14; 2 CORINTHIANS 3:17–18

In the beginning was the Word, and the Word was with God, and the Word was God. He was in the beginning with God. All things were made through him, and without him was not any thing made that was made. In him was life, and the life was the light of men. . . .

And the Word became flesh and dwelt among us, and we have seen his glory, glory as of the only Son from the Father, full of grace and truth.

Now the Lord is the Spirit, and where the Spirit of the Lord is, there is freedom. And we all, with unveiled face, beholding the glory of the Lord, are being transformed into the same image from one degree of glory to another.

✤ HYMNS

"Jesus, Priceless Treasure"
"Turn Your Eyes upon Jesus"

ENDLESS LOVE

✤ CALL TO CONFESSION: DEUTERONOMY
10:12–13, 15; HOSEA 6:4, 6–7

"And now, Israel, what does the LORD your God require of you, but to fear the LORD your God, to walk in all his ways, to love him, to serve the LORD your God with all your heart and with all your soul, and to keep the commandments and statutes of the LORD, which I am commanding you today for your good? . . . The LORD set his heart in love on your fathers and chose their offspring after them, you above all peoples, as you are this day."

❖❖❖

What shall I do with you, O Ephraim?
    What shall I do with you, O Judah?
Your love is like a morning cloud,
    like the dew that goes early away.

. . . .

For I desire steadfast love and not sacrifice,
    the knowledge of God rather than burnt offerings.

But like Adam they transgressed the covenant;
    there they dealt faithlessly with me.

✤ PRAYER OF CONFESSION

Faithful Father, heavenly Husband,

Your love for us is changeless and unending. We confess that our love for you is weak, flickering, variable, and laced with selfish ambition and desire. Your love is like a mighty ocean that rushes toward us each day and envelops us with kindness, mercy, and steadfast faithfulness. Our love for you is like a fleeting mist: a vapor that rises from time to time and quickly evaporates in the heat of life's pain and suffering. Father, forgive us for loving so many other gods and giving our lives to them, while failing to notice your hand of love at work for us each day. You govern the entire universe and work all things together for our good, but we are quick to blame you, to turn away from you, and to give our worship and love to many other husbands. Lord, forgive us for our many sins.

Jesus, thank you for your changeless and unending love. You loved us before the foundation of the world and entered history in order to redeem us. As a human being, you loved God and your neighbor perfectly, loving and serving God and keeping every one of his statutes and commandments. You did this because you knew that we never could, and so you gave us the gift of your spotless perfection.

Holy Spirit, fill us with gratitude for the love we have in Christ that will never let us go. Though our sins are many and increase in number every day, lift up our heads and show us the cross. We thank you that we cannot close our hearts to you, for your love is relentless, and in faithfulness you pursue us and draw us back to you time and time again. Show us the beauty of our beloved husband, Jesus Christ: his wounds that paid our ransom and his faithful obedience that makes us perfect in him. Help us to love and cherish him in growing obedience until we bow before him at last and sing his praises for all eternity. Even so, come quickly, Lord Jesus. Amen.

✤ ASSURANCE OF PARDON: REVELATION 19:6–9

Then I heard what seemed to be the voice of a great multitude, like the roar of many waters and like the sound of mighty peals of thunder, crying out,

> "Hallelujah!
> For the Lord our God
>   the Almighty reigns.
> Let us rejoice and exult
>   and give him the glory,
> for the marriage of the Lamb has come,
>   and his Bride has made herself ready;
> it was granted her to clothe herself
>   with fine linen, bright and pure"—

for the fine linen is the righteous deeds of the saints.

And the angel said to me, "Write this: Blessed are those who are invited to the marriage supper of the Lamb." And he said to me, "These are the true words of God."

✣ HYMNS

"Jesus, Thy Blood and Righteousness"
"O Love That Will Not Let Me Go"

FOOLISHNESS

✤ CALL TO CONFESSION: PSALM 14:1–3;
   EPHESIANS 5:15–17

The fool says in his heart, "There is no God."
>   They are corrupt, they do abominable deeds;
>   there is none who does good.

The Lord looks down from heaven on the children of
>   man,
>   to see if there are any who understand,
>   who seek after God.

They have all turned aside; together they have become
>   corrupt;
>   there is none who does good,
>   not even one.

Look carefully then how you walk, not as unwise but as wise, making the best use of the time, because the days are evil. Therefore do not be foolish, but understand what the will of the Lord is.

✤ PRAYER OF CONFESSION

Our wise and loving Father,

We admit to you our foolishness and habitual blindness to your will. We often believe that we are wiser and more loving than you are, and we try to use prayer to manipulate you into doing what we want. We are full of turmoil and anxiety because we do not trust in your wisdom or believe that all your ways are best for us. We do not walk carefully through life, making the best use of our time, because we are consumed with worshipping idols that will never satisfy our cravings. Although we claim to believe in you and fear you, we spend most of our days living as though you do not exist. We rarely think of you or run to you with our cares and burdens, but we frantically try to fix our problems according to our own foolish thinking. We forget to worship you throughout each day because we cannot see your loving, sovereign kindness wrapped around us even in our most painful moments. Father, forgive us for our functional atheism.

Thank you for loving profoundly foolish and sinful rebels like us. You sent your cherished Son to live among blind and evil people so that we could be rescued from our foolish depravity. He lived the perfect life of obedience and faith, demonstrating your wisdom for us in living proof with each word and action. On the cross he submitted to your gracious plan, choosing to pay for all of our blind iniquity, sin upon sin. Now we stand before you as perfectly wise and righteous children, even though we will continue to struggle with blind foolishness until we see you face to face. For this gift of Christ's righteousness, we are eternally grateful.

Patient and persistent God, we thank you that we cannot change ourselves from the fools that we are by nature. If we could, we would take credit for our discernment and despise our brothers and sisters who are more foolish than we are. Instead, you have made us completely dependent on you for every true thought and good deed so that we can boast only in you. Thank you for promising to complete the good work you have begun in us, even against our will. Please soften our hard hearts and open our blind eyes more each day. Help us to see our sin clearly, to see you clearly, and to long to grow in wisdom. Give us strong faith to believe that you love us passionately and will work for our good in all things. Keep us near the cross, always needy and looking to you for mercy and hope. Fill us with your wisdom and be our vision, our battle shield, our dignity, and our delight until the day when we see you with new eyes. Amen.

✤ ASSURANCE OF PARDON: EPHESIANS 1:16–21

I do not cease to give thanks for you, remembering you in my prayers, that the God of our Lord Jesus Christ, the Father of glory, may give you the Spirit of wisdom and of revelation in the knowledge of him, having the eyes of your hearts enlightened, that you may know what is the hope to which he has called you, what are the riches of his glorious inheritance in the saints, and what is the immeasurable greatness of his power toward us who believe, according to the working of his great might that he worked in Christ when he raised him from the dead and seated him at his right hand in the heavenly places, far above all rule and authority and power and dominion, and above every name that is named, not only in this age but also in the one to come.

✦ HYMNS

"God, Be Merciful to Me"
"I'll Rest in Christ"
"Be Thou My Vision"

GOD'S LAW

✢ CALL TO CONFESSION: PSALM 19:7–10; ROMANS 7:22–24

The law of the LORD is perfect,
　reviving the soul;
the testimony of the LORD is sure,
　making wise the simple;
the precepts of the LORD are right,
　rejoicing the heart;
the commandment of the LORD is pure,
　enlightening the eyes;
the fear of the LORD is clean,
　enduring forever;
the rules of the LORD are true,
　and righteous altogether.
More to be desired are they than gold,
　even much fine gold;
sweeter also than honey
　and drippings of the honeycomb.

✢✢✢

For I delight in the law of God, in my inner being, but I see in my members another law waging war against the law of my mind and making me captive to the law of sin that dwells in my members. Wretched man that I am! Who will deliver me from this body of death?

✢ PRAYER OF CONFESSION

Holy Father,

You are our great and glorious Creator. You have graciously given your perfect and wise law as a lamp to guide our steps. Every part of your creation delights to do your holy will—except for us. Lord, our love of sin astounds us. Whether we have known you for many years or are babies in the faith, it is our nature to sin. Our affections are turned away from you, and none of our desires or motivations are pure. Though we have died to the eternal consequences of our sin, we daily choose to live as slaves to lust and selfishness, doing things we know that we shouldn't and failing to do the things that we know that we should. We medicate ourselves against pain in many sinful ways, and our minds are full of dark imaginings. We continually try to patch together our own rags of righteousness, to prove to you that we are worth loving, worth saving, worth keeping. Father, have mercy on us.

Jesus, though our sins are vast in number, your grace is greater still! You are our Rock and our Redeemer and have provided everything necessary for our salvation. Though our guilt rises to the heavens to condemn us, your righteousness soars above it to plead on our behalf. Each of our sins is paid for, past, present, and future, and your perfect record of holiness is credited to us, as if we had never sinned. Thank you.

Holy Spirit, melt our hearts with the reality of how we have been cherished in Christ. Help us not to use grace as an excuse to sin more. Instead, delight and ravish us with the love of our Savior until our hearts change and we desire him, and obedience to him, above everything else. May the outrageous joy of the gospel free us to keep trying to put off sin and put on obedience, knowing that Christ's goodness in our place is all that we need in order to win your approval.

Thank you that we will not be like this forever. Although in this world we will make only small beginnings in truly loving your law, a day is coming when we will be new creations, inside and out, and will stand before you in sinless perfection. O God, until that day, may the sweet rest that we have in the work of Christ give us fresh courage and strength to engage the daily battle with our sinful hearts, with gratitude and joy. In the strong name of Jesus Christ we pray, amen.

✤ ASSURANCE OF PARDON: GALATIANS 4:4–7

When the fullness of time had come, God sent forth his Son, born of woman, born under the law, to redeem those who were under the law, so that we might receive adoption as sons. And because you are sons, God has sent the Spirit of his Son into our hearts, crying, "Abba! Father!" So you are no longer a slave, but a son, and if a son, then an heir through God.

✤ HYMNS

"Arise, My Soul, Arise"
"Jesus Paid It All"

CLEAN HANDS

✤ CALL TO CONFESSION: PSALM 24:3–5

> Who shall ascend the hill of the LORD?
>> And who shall stand in his holy place?
> He who has clean hands and a pure heart,
>> who does not lift up his soul to what is false
>> and does not swear deceitfully.
> He will receive blessing from the LORD
>> and righteousness from the God of his salvation.

✤ PRAYER OF CONFESSION

Glorious heavenly Father,

We admit that we don't see your glory very clearly. In heaven we will be captivated by your beauty, but now we are weak and sinful and do not adore you as we should. We do not have clean hands and pure hearts, but have wandered away like lost sheep. Our idolatrous hearts desire many things besides you; our days are filled with other thoughts; we live in a world full of strong temptations and have an enemy who knows how to draw our eyes away from you. Father, forgive us for finding so much glory in your creation while failing to see you in all of your wonder and radiant majesty. Our souls are darkened and all our motives mixed, yet you allowed your perfect Son to die in our place. Help us to see the great glory of your love and forgiveness through the outrageous sacrifice of the cross.

Jesus, you preserved purity in both your heart and your hands. You touched lepers and brought them wholeness instead of becoming defiled by them; you ate with tax collectors and sinners and called them away from their sin rather than being drawn into sin by them. You used your hands to glorify and praise your Father, and now you have ascended into the heavenly sanctuary, which you purified once for all with your own blood. Now you grant us access to the Father through the gift of your perfect cleanliness—what a privilege is ours!

Holy Spirit, open our eyes to see the magnificence of our

great Savior. Lovingly strip away the idols and trinkets that seem so priceless to us, yet keep us from worshiping him alone. Wean us from our strong attachments to your wonderful gifts, and quiet our anxious thoughts when you take them away. When we see our impure hearts and unclean hands, give us the gifts of godly sorrow and swift repentance. May the darkness of our sin magnify the glory of Jesus Christ, whose perfect heart and spotless hands have been credited to us. Make us grateful that through him we are worthy to belong to the King of Glory, to fall at his feet and join in worshiping him forever. Until then, may we live as joyful and grateful debtors to your mercy alone. In Jesus' name we pray, amen.

✤ ASSURANCE OF PARDON: EZEKIEL 36:25–27

"I will sprinkle clean water on you, and you shall be clean from all your uncleannesses, and from all your idols I will cleanse you. And I will give you a new heart, and a new spirit I will put within you. And I will remove the heart of stone from your flesh and give you a heart of flesh. And I will put my Spirit within you, and cause you to walk in my statutes and be careful to obey my rules."

✤ HYMNS

"A Debtor to Mercy"
"Beneath the Cross of Jesus"

PATIENCE

❖ CALL TO CONFESSION: PSALM 37:30–34

The mouth of the righteous utters wisdom,
   and his tongue speaks justice.
The law of his God is in his heart;
   his steps do not slip.

The wicked watches for the righteous
   and seeks to put him to death.
The LORD will not abandon him to his power
   or let him be condemned when he is brought to trial.

Wait for the LORD and keep his way,
   and he will exalt you to inherit the land;
   you will look on when the wicked are cut off.

❖ PRAYER OF CONFESSION

Righteous heavenly Father,
   We confess that we are often agitated by the evil we see in ourselves and others. In our sin and weakness, we find it difficult to trust you and act kindly. Instead, we hold onto rage, fretting with fear and imagining ways to get even with those who sin against us. Our thoughts are disturbed—dissecting, criticizing, despising, and plotting. Sometimes we lash out in anger, wounding others with our deeds and words. Sometimes we withdraw in cold hatred, punishing others with our disdain and rejection. Either way, we struggle to believe that you will act and that you are for us. We are tempted to envy unrighteous people and covet their apparent freedom and prosperity. We forget that you are strong and good and that you love to save and protect your people. Lord, if we could trust you with our welfare, we would be free to love others in their weakness. If we could be patient and wait for you to act, we would enjoy greater peace. If we could be satisfied with you and what you have given, we could be generous to others instead of envious.

Father, forgive us for our great sin and weakness. Have mercy on us.

Lord, thank you for your great patience and love toward us. We have drunk deeply from the gushing fountains of your forgiveness and generosity, and we marvel that we can still be so vengeful, stingy, and full of malice toward others. Thank you for uniting us to your Son and giving us his perfect faith and patience, his love for evil people, his lack of fear and selfishness, his refusal to covet or envy, his perfect anger and perfect peace, his lavish generosity with his life, time, and love—all credited to us! Help us to take delight in him and cherish him.

Holy Spirit, we need your help every moment of every day. We can't see our hateful, envious, impatient selves without your guidance, and we cannot change our hearts. Show us our hearts and give us grace to face evil in ourselves and others with patience, honesty, compassion, and the same forgiveness that we have received in Christ. When we succeed, make us thankful so that we give all the glory to you alone. When we fail and fall, help us to repent and see the radiance of Christ in our place, and make us thankful. May our failures lead us to worship the only One who never failed and who gladly lived and died for us in order to share his grand inheritance with us forever. Amen.

✤ ASSURANCE OF PARDON: TITUS 3:4–7

But when the goodness and loving kindness of God our Savior appeared, he saved us, not because of works done by us in righteousness, but according to his own mercy, by the washing of regeneration and renewal of the Holy Spirit, whom he poured out on us richly through Jesus Christ our Savior, so that being justified by his grace we might become heirs according to the hope of eternal life.

✤ HYMNS

"Out of the Depths"
"Higher Throne"

A SHELTER
IN THE STORM

✤ **CALL TO CONFESSION: PSALM 46:1–3**

God is our refuge and strength,
a very present help in trouble.
Therefore we will not fear though the earth gives way,
though the mountains be moved into the heart of the
sea,
though its waters roar and foam,
though the mountains tremble at its swelling.

✤ **PRAYER OF CONFESSION**

Infinitely wise God,

Your wisdom is unsearchable and infinite; your arm is powerful and mighty; your will is sovereign throughout this universe; your patience and love for fallen sinners like us defy our understanding. Lord, we can do nothing but sin, and each new day demonstrates that we are lovers of darkness, covenant breakers, and full of fear. We have received unfathomable mercy and abundant grace, yet we frequently trample on your beloved Son by cherishing anxious thoughts and living in fear of those around us. Instead of believing that you are a secure refuge in whom we can hide, we imagine a thousand scenarios of pain and loss. Instead of trusting that you are a present help who will defend us, we pursue our own revenge against those who have hurt us. We harbor bitterness toward you in our hearts over our problems, real and imagined, and we punish others in a variety of sinful ways for hurting us: by coldness and silence, by malice and slander, by rehearsing our grievances and nurturing our grudges. O God, forgive us for the overwhelming fear that dwells in our hearts and damages our relationship with you and with others.

Lord Jesus, without your righteousness we would be perpetually undone. We cannot imagine the beauty of your sinless heart when you prayed for the forgiveness of those who were killing you, but we thank you for it. We cannot fathom the depth of your trust in your heavenly Father, even as he turned his face away from you at the cross. Your blood washes us clean, and your obedience covers our endless record of disobedience. Thank you for the deep love and mercy that led you to pity us and to give your own life to save ours.

Holy Spirit, lead us to repentance and save us from despair. Give us grace to see our sin clearly and to come to you renouncing ourselves, hating our sin, and hoping fully in the forgiveness that flows even to us, the chiefs of sinners. Drive the joy of our salvation deep into our hearts, until trusting you feels like the only thing we can do. Give us hearts that seek reconciliation and peace with those who have hurt us, even when doing so is costly and painful to us. Help us to turn away from evil and to repay it with love and kindness; help us to love as we have been loved in Christ. Taking refuge in Jesus' strong name, we pray: amen.

✤ ASSURANCE OF PARDON: PSALM 46:4–11

> There is a river whose streams make glad the city of God,
>> the holy habitation of the Most High.
> God is in the midst of her; she shall not be moved;
>> God will help her when morning dawns.
> The nations rage, the kingdoms totter;
>> he utters his voice, the earth melts.
> The LORD of hosts is with us;
>> the God of Jacob is our fortress.
>
> Come, behold the works of the LORD,
>> how he has brought desolations on the earth.
> He makes wars cease to the end of the earth;
>> he breaks the bow and shatters the spear;
>> he burns the chariots with fire.
> "Be still, and know that I am God.
>> I will be exalted among the nations,
>> I will be exalted in the earth!"

The LORD of hosts is with us;
the God of Jacob is our fortress.

✤ HYMNS

"Abide with Me"
"A Mighty Fortress"

GOD, OUR WARRIOR

✣ **CALL TO CONFESSION: PSALM 55:17–18**

> Evening and morning and at noon
>> I utter my complaint and moan,
>> and he hears my voice.
> He redeems my soul in safety
>> from the battle that I wage,
>> for many are arrayed against me.

✣ **PRAYER OF CONFESSION**

Mighty God,

The forces that are arrayed against us in this life far outmatch our little strength. We do not wrestle against flesh and blood but against powerful spiritual forces in the heavenly realms. Our enemy is strong and crafty, and if we try to stand against him in our own strength we will inevitably fail. Yet, Father, we confess that we often trust in our own wisdom and strength, as if we were mighty and self-sufficient. We go through life oblivious to the dangers around us and not heeding the warnings of your Word. When we find ourselves defeated yet again, we complain and moan as if you had let us down, when the fault is entirely ours. Instead of praying and asking for your help, we grumble and resent our weakness. Father, forgive us.

Jesus, thank you that you have entered the battle on our behalf, leaving the safety of heaven to engage the challenges of living as a human being. You felt all of our human weaknesses, yet you endured without sin, because you constantly entrusted yourself to your Father's mighty power. Thank you that you were triumphant for us, redeeming us and giving our souls complete safety in you. The strong forces that are arrayed against us can never separate us from you, and so our ultimate victory is secure.

Holy Spirit, thank you that you are at work strengthening us daily. When you give us the grace to stand, depending upon you, help us to remember that the strength is yours and not ours. When you leave us to ourselves and we fall, show us your good purposes in that, too—help us to learn our own weakness, to become more watchful and distrustful of ourselves, to pray more frequently and fervently, and to become more eager for the final day of our victory in Christ. Thank you that he is even now interceding for us and that he will continue to do so throughout our earthly warfare, until he welcomes us into his closer presence. In Jesus' name we pray, amen.

✤ ASSURANCE OF PARDON: ROMANS 8:37–39; REVELATION 3:21

In all these things we are more than conquerors through him who loved us. For I am sure that neither death nor life, nor angels nor rulers, nor things present nor things to come, nor powers, nor height nor depth, nor anything else in all creation, will be able to separate us from the love of God in Christ Jesus our Lord.

"The one who conquers, I will grant him to sit with me on my throne, as I also conquered and sat down with my Father on his throne."

✤ HYMNS

"How High and How Wide"
"Nothing That My Hands Can Do"

WAITING (1)

❖ CALL TO CONFESSION: PSALM 62:1–2; 69:3; 27:14

> For God alone my soul waits in silence;
> > from him comes my salvation.
> He alone is my rock and my salvation,
> > my fortress; I shall not be greatly shaken.

❖❖❖

> I am weary with my crying out;
> > my throat is parched.
> My eyes grow dim
> > with waiting for my God.

❖❖❖

> Wait for the LORD;
> > be strong, and let your heart take courage;
> wait for the LORD!

❖ PRAYER OF CONFESSION

Loving heavenly Father,

We ask that, by your Spirit, you would help us to admit what is true about ourselves: that we have no goodness of our own and need the goodness of Jesus Christ to cover us. We are undeserving of your passionate love and are full of sinful desires, but you are full of grace. We are restless and impatient, grasping what we crave instead of trusting that you love us and enjoy showering your precious children with good gifts. We find it hard to wait for you to answer our prayers, to give us what we want, to relieve our suffering, to fulfill our dreams. Every part of us—our souls, minds, and bodies—is corrupted with selfishness. We are fallen and twisted, and there is a fountain of pollution deep within our nature. We are deeply ashamed of the depravity that clings to us and the sin that we cherish in secret. The truth of your Word reveals who we are, striking a heavy blow at our pride and leaving us in pieces before you. We confess our frequent and willful sin to you. Father, forgive us.

But you have given us another master and Lord: your son, Jesus Christ. He waited patiently for your will in all things and never gave in to the enticing temptations that surrounded him. He loved sinners without participating in their sin, and freely forgave the most notorious people while waiting in purity for his own wedding day. Now we stand dressed in the spectacular robes of his perfect goodness, with a record of complete purity that we could never earn. Jesus, we are undone by your patient, persistent love for weak sinners like us.

Holy Spirit, teach us to guard our hearts and minds as we wait. Fill us with gratitude and love; strengthen our desires for obedience and purity. Help us to love you, our triune God, with all of our hearts, bodies, minds and souls, for we are weak and cannot do that well. Help us to trust in the generous loving-kindness of our Father and to value his wisdom more than our own. When we fail, help us to hide away in Christ, cherishing his obedience in our place. Help us to wait joyfully for the day when all waiting will be over, when we will see our beloved Savior and be fully joined to him forever. For the glory of Jesus Christ we pray, amen.

✤ ASSURANCE OF PARDON: PSALM 25:6–8; 40:1–3

> Remember your mercy, O LORD, and your steadfast love,
>   for they have been from of old.
> Remember not the sins of my youth or my transgressions;
>   according to your steadfast love remember me,
>   for the sake of your goodness, O LORD!
>
> Good and upright is the LORD;
>   therefore he instructs sinners in the way.

✤✤✤

> I waited patiently for the LORD;
>   he inclined to me and heard my cry.

He drew me up from the pit of destruction,
  out of the miry bog,
and set my feet upon a rock,
  making my steps secure.
He put a new song in my mouth,
  a song of praise to our God.
Many will see and fear,
  and put their trust in the Lord.

✥ HYMNS

"All I Have Is Christ"
"Jesus, Be My All (How Sad Our State)"

GOD'S MAJESTY

✤ CALL TO CONFESSION: PSALM 99:1–3

The LORD reigns; let the peoples tremble!
>He sits enthroned upon the cherubim; let the earth
>>quake!
The LORD is great in Zion;
>he is exalted over all the peoples.
Let them praise your great and awesome name!
>Holy is he!

✤ PRAYER OF CONFESSION

Glorious and holy God,
>You are far beyond our knowledge, yet eager to be known by us; mysterious, yet revealed to us in your creation, your Word, and your Son; radiant in holiness and glory, yet merciful to your wayward children. You deserve praise and honor, for you are the King of Kings and Lord of Lords, and at your pleasure empires rise and fall.

>What did you see in us, that we—diseased and despised sinners—should be clothed in your bright glory? That fallen rebels like us should be lifted from a pit of sin to be seated next to a king? That those who are groaning, weeping, and grumbling should be invited to a joy as full as our hearts can hold? Who can fathom such immeasurable love?

>Father, teach us to honor and fear you as we should. You are a powerful God and consuming fire. Forgive us for our tendency to treat you as our errand boy and good luck charm, whose job it is to serve us and do our bidding. Forgive us for fearing you sinfully, for our failure to trust you, for mistaking your hand of love and instruction for a fist of vengeance and anger, for doubting that you have poured out all your wrath on Christ in our place. Father, forgive us and help us to understand your heart—to worship you with holy reverence and great joy.

>Holy Spirit, comfort us often with the righteousness of Christ. We have been given a glorious record of obedience we

could never earn; let us see his childlike trust and respect for his Father, his deep humility, and his utter dependence on God. Show us that all of his goodness has been given to us and covers us, though we struggle daily to rest in his grace and mercy. May we be diligent to honor and serve the one who has suffered in our place. Help us to see our sin, to mourn for it, and then to dance and frolic in the finished work of Christ. Ravish us with his glory, inflame our hearts with love and gratitude, and transform our sluggish and tepid souls until we are fervent with joy and devoted to obedience. May the unfathomable beauty of Christ and his immeasurable love for us cause us to burn with holy fear and boundless delight until we see his face and fall at his feet in worship. In his glorious name we pray, amen.

✤ ASSURANCE OF PARDON: ISAIAH 57:15

For thus says the One who is high and lifted up,
    who inhabits eternity, whose name is Holy:
"I dwell in the high and holy place,
    and also with him who is of a contrite and lowly spirit,
to revive the spirit of the lowly,
    and to revive the heart of the contrite."

✤ HYMNS

"Behold Our God"
"Poor Sinner Dejected with Fear"

HIDING FROM GOD

✤ CALL TO CONFESSION: PSALM 119:1–3, 70:4–5

Blessed are those whose way is blameless,
    who walk in the law of the LORD!
Blessed are those who keep his testimonies,
    who seek him with their whole heart,
who also do no wrong,
    but walk in his ways!

May all who seek you
    rejoice and be glad in you!
May those who love your salvation
    say evermore, "God is great!"
But I am poor and needy;
    hasten to me, O God!
You are my help and my deliverer;
    O LORD, do not delay!

✤ PRAYER OF CONFESSION

Lover of our souls,

Like Adam and Eve, we are people who hide from you instead of running toward you when we sin. In the footsteps of our fallen parents, we idolize your good creation and use it to escape from you, fashioning pathetic fig leaves and hiding behind the bushes that you have made. We seek our own glory instead of yours, craving comfort, good reputations, financial gain, safety, significance, and love. We want to believe that we are the smartest, the best, the wisest, the strongest, and the most spiritual people. We compete with one another in order to feel superior, and we trample each other with our pride and determination to succeed. We have never sought you with our whole hearts, though we daily pursue our own desires with all of our heart, mind, soul, and strength. Lord, forgive us for our relentless self-love and worship.

Holy Spirit, show us that we are poor, weak, and needy. Come quickly to deliver us from our blindness and to rescue us from our pride and shame. Help us to see the many lovers we embrace as we run from you. Convict us of our sin and give us the sweet gifts of repentance and godly sorrow. Show us our sinless Savior, who always obeyed his Father, seeking the Father's will and glory above his own comfort and safety. In the garden of Gethsemane he agonized, longing to escape the bitter shame and curse of the death appointed for him. Yet he sought us with his whole heart by living and dying for us, rising triumphantly to claim us for himself, and fulfilling his Father's purpose to have a beloved people of his own.

Fill our hearts and minds with the reality of Christ's loving pursuit of us, so that we learn to love him more each day. Help us to be filled constantly with gratitude to him, to love him more than we love our pathetic idols, to seek him with growing joy, to run to him swiftly when we sin, and to have unshakeable confidence in his finished work and his perpetual care for us. In Jesus' name we pray, amen.

✦ ASSURANCE OF PARDON: LUKE 15:1–7, ROMANS 5:8–9

Now the tax collectors and sinners were all drawing near to hear him. And the Pharisees and the scribes grumbled, saying, "This man receives sinners and eats with them."

So he told them this parable: "What man of you, having a hundred sheep, if he has lost one of them, does not leave the ninety-nine in the open country, and go after the one that is lost, until he finds it? And when he has found it, he lays it on his shoulders, rejoicing. And when he comes home, he calls together his friends and his neighbors, saying to them, 'Rejoice with me, for I have found my sheep that was lost.' Just so, I tell you, there will be more joy in heaven over one sinner who repents than over ninety-nine righteous persons who need no repentance."

✤✤✤

God shows his love for us in that while we were still sinners, Christ died for us. Since, therefore, we have now been justified by his blood, much more shall we be saved by him from the wrath of God.

✤ HYMNS

"O Come, O Come, Emmanuel"
"You Are My All in All"

HOPE DEFERRED

✤ CALL TO CONFESSION: PROVERBS 13:12

Hope deferred makes the heart sick,
but a desire fulfilled is a tree of life.

✤ PRAYER OF CONFESSION

Lord Jesus,

Thank you for becoming one of us so we could know that you understand what it feels like to live in a fallen and terrifying world. You know what it is to have a heart sick with sorrow at the death of a dear friend, a soul consumed with agony and dread at the prospect of suffering, a body that is ill and unable to function, and a heart betrayed by those who profess loyalty— you were used by others for what you could do for them, misunderstood and falsely accused, rejected and despised though you were innocent. You could have stayed in heaven, blissfully untouched by the foulest aspects of sin and depravity, but you chose to enter into the chaos for the sake of loving us and dying for us. Now you love us patiently and walk along with us as we experience those things as well. You comfort us, strengthen us, and protect us with the shining gift of your perfect obedience in all things, carefully measuring out times of joy and strength with times of difficulty and sadness to help us grow.

Jesus, remind us of your suffering and love often. We are easily overwhelmed by the very real sorrows and challenges that come from our own sinful hearts, the sins of others, and the ordinary sorrows and burdens of living in this world that is out of our control. We are consumed by fear of things real and imaginary, and in our fear we sin a great deal to try to manage situations or escape from them for a brief moment. We often forget how kind and patient you are and how you are very much in control. We forget your promises; we forget the ways you have cared for us in the past; we behave as though you don't exist or don't care. We live life as practical atheists, in spite of what we claim to believe. Lord, forgive us for this very great rejection of you.

Lord, help us in our weakness. When darkness hides your lovely face, may we know, just as surely as we know that the sun will shine again, that you are there, presiding on your throne, ruling the universe, and working all things together for the good of those who love you. Help us to grow toward remembering that truth and toward trusting you in the bleakest times, confident that no matter what we see or imagine around us, you are true reality and are always for us. Teach us to wait with greater confidence that you do all things well. Remind us of the day that is coming, when all our desires will find their fulfillment in your presence and when hope will finally become reality. Encourage us with glimpses of the joy that will soon be ours so that we can walk faithfully through the troubled days that you call us to live in. In your strong name we pray, amen.

❖ ASSURANCE OF PARDON: ROMANS 5:1–2; 8:24–25

Therefore, since we have been justified by faith, we have peace with God through our Lord Jesus Christ. Through him we have also obtained access by faith into this grace in which we stand, and we rejoice in hope of the glory of God.

For in this hope we were saved. Now hope that is seen is not hope. For who hopes for what he sees? But if we hope for what we do not see, we wait for it with patience.

❖ HYMNS

"Jesus, My Only Hope"
"Out of the Depths"

STRAYING SHEEP

✤ CALL TO CONFESSION: ISAIAH 53:6

All we like sheep have gone astray;
  we have turned—every one—to his own way;
and the LORD has laid on him
  the iniquity of us all.

✤ PRAYER OF CONFESSION

Loving heavenly Father,

We have wild and rebellious hearts. We claim to value your wisdom above our own, but we are weak and blinded by our own sin. When you walk us through frightening valleys, we quickly turn aside like foolish sheep to comfort ourselves with sin, instead of believing that you love us and will always provide what we need. When we don't like the path ahead because it is hard and stony, we refuse to follow you and accuse you of not caring. Though you satisfy our souls with good things, we have little appetite for the feast to which you call us. Our desire for your Word is weak; we do not love worshiping with your people as we should; our hearts are without affection for you; our minds are easily captivated by temptations that dazzle us far more than your love amazes us; and even our repentance is tinged with pride and selfishness. Father, forgive us. Lord, have mercy on us in our great weakness. Thank you for your endless patience with your wandering children and for covering us in the righteousness of your Son.

Jesus, you are both the sinless Lamb of God and the Great Shepherd who gave his life for us. Thank you for following your Father and for never straying off the path of obedience even when Satan tempted you in every way. Thank you for paying for our sin and for giving us your perfect goodness as a free gift through faith. Thank you for walking through the valley of death's shadow for us and for promising to walk through it with us when you lead us there. Thank you for interceding for us before your Father's throne and for your promise to hold on to us and lead us safely home.

Holy Spirit, press the gospel deep into our hearts, and change our disordered affections. Engage our rebellious wills so that we want what you want and long to obey you more than we desire to sin. Strengthen us to stand in obedience when our hearts do desire to follow you. May we never use grace as an excuse to sin more freely. Make Christ beautiful to us until we are so captivated by his love, mercy, patience, and kindness that we are undone and eager to follow him wherever he leads. Rescue us time and time again from our fallen natures, until the day when they will be gone forever and we will gather around your throne to hail you as our matchless King through all eternity. In the name of Jesus Christ we pray, amen.

✤ ASSURANCE OF PARDON: EZEKIEL 34:11–12; JOHN 10:11, 27–28

"For thus says the Lord God: Behold, I, I myself will search for my sheep and will seek them out. As a shepherd seeks out his flock when he is among his sheep that have been scattered, so will I seek out my sheep, and I will rescue them from all places where they have been scattered on a day of clouds and thick darkness."

[Jesus said,] "I am the good shepherd. The good shepherd lays down his life for the sheep. . . ."

". . . My sheep hear my voice, and I know them, and they follow me. I give them eternal life, and they will never perish, and no one will snatch them out of my hand."

✤ HYMNS

"Come, Thou Fount of Every Blessing"
"Crown Him with Many Crowns"
"None Other Lamb"

SPIRITUAL DISCIPLINES

✤ CALL TO CONFESSION: ISAIAH 58:1–4; LUKE 18:11–13

"Declare to my people their transgression,
    to the house of Jacob their sins.
Yet they seek me daily
    and delight to know my ways,
as if they were a nation that did righteousness
    and did not forsake the judgment of their God;
they ask of me righteous judgments;
    they delight to draw near to God.
'Why have we fasted, and you see it not?
    Why have we humbled ourselves, and you take no
        knowledge of it?'
Behold, in the day of your fast you seek your own pleasure,
    and oppress all your workers.
Behold, you fast only to quarrel and to fight
    and to hit with a wicked fist.
Fasting like yours this day
    will not make your voice to be heard on high."

"The Pharisee, standing by himself, prayed thus: 'God, I thank you that I am not like other men, extortioners, unjust, adulterers, or even like this tax collector. I fast twice a week; I give tithes of all that I get.' But the tax collector, standing far off, would not even lift up his eyes to heaven, but beat his breast, saying, 'God, be merciful to me, a sinner!'"

✤ PRAYER OF CONFESSION

Triune God,
    Help us to recognize and repent from our many sins. We confess that we have treasured many things above our Savior,

and have nurtured storehouses of idols that call for our worship. We have been elated when they smiled upon us, and cast down and depressed when they cursed us, instead of looking to you and basking in your unchangeable love. Sometimes we have even made an idol out of our spiritual disciplines: our Bible study, our prayer, our fasting, our service of others. Forgive us for finding our salvation, joy, and identity in our strengths. Teach us instead to delight in and feast upon all the spiritual treasure you have lavished on us so richly in Christ: the banquet of his righteousness given to us, the abundant riches of his grace and kindness poured out on us, the glorious inheritance he has earned for us by his perfect obedience and death. Teach us to humble ourselves and repent properly, with broken hearts and not merely outward show. Remind us often who we are in Christ, as we walk through a world of temptation that dazzles and beckons us. Draw our hearts and minds to the cross daily so we will marvel at your purposeful and determined love for starving beggars like us, who have nothing to give you but our sin. Help us not to be undone by our sin, but to be driven by it to delight all the more in your rich mercy and grace.

Gracious Redeemer, thank you for your patience that has borne with us so long. Thank you for perfectly feasting, and entering into the joys of life here on earth, alongside those who rejoice. Thank you too for mourning and fasting perfectly alongside those who weep. Unite us to yourself with inseparable bonds, so that nothing may ever draw us back from you. Help us to grow in putting on genuine righteousness without ever trusting in it to win your favor. Keep us grounded in your truth throughout the challenging times in which we live, until that day when we finally see the glorious things that you have prepared for those who believe. That day will be all feasting—the end of fasting, praying, pleading, mourning, humbling, watching, fearing, and sinning. Teach us to long for that last day, and lead us to it soon. In Jesus' name, amen.

✤ ASSURANCE OF PARDON: JOEL 2:12–13

"Yet even now," declares the LORD,
    "return to me with all your heart,

with fasting, with weeping, and with mourning;
    and rend your hearts and not your garments."
Return to the LORD your God,
    for he is gracious and merciful,
slow to anger, and abounding in steadfast love;
    and he relents over disaster.

✤ HYMNS

"Great Is Thy Faithfulness"
"Nothing That My Hands Can Do"

RIGHTEOUSNESS

✤ CALL TO CONFESSION: ISAIAH 64:6

> We have all become like one who is unclean,
>   and all our righteous deeds are like a polluted garment.
> We all fade like a leaf,
>   and our iniquities, like the wind, take us away.

✤ PRAYER OF CONFESSION

Holy Lord,

We are not fit to come before you. We have no righteousness of our own to offer, and we possess nothing to sacrifice that is worthy of the great debt that we owe you. We have not done what is just and right, but instead have frequently sinned in our words and our actions. We have not loved kindness and delighted our souls in doing others good. Instead, we have delighted in harming those whom we deem our enemies, and even when we have done good to others, we have resented them in our hearts. We have not walked humbly and wisely before you, but rather we have walked in our own wisdom and followed the counsel of the world around us. Father, forgive us.

Jesus, you are our righteousness, and you have made the perfect offering to atone for our sin. You walked humbly with God every day of your life, you loved faithfulness and mercy, and you burned for justice. These glorious attributes are our only hope of entering God's presence, yet we wanted you dead because of them, and so we crucified you. What great arrogance, hatred of kindness, and injustice belongs to our race—and to us as well! Thank you for your great mercy in which you come to sinners like us, cleanse us with your precious blood, and clothe us in your perfect righteousness. Hallelujah! What a Savior you are!

Holy Spirit, work in us true righteousness. Take away our hard and stony hearts and create in us true goodness and beauty. Give us a new desire to walk in your statutes and to live by your rules, out of the thankfulness of our hearts for our rich salvation. Give us deep and abiding joy in the gospel—a joy that neither our circumstances nor our sin can take away. Fix our eyes increasingly on the everlasting inheritance of righteousness that is ours in Christ—on the new heavens and the new earth where we shall finally be able to enter your presence, by your grace alone, standing on the righteousness of Christ alone. In Jesus' holy name we pray, amen.

❖ ASSURANCE OF PARDON: JEREMIAH 23:5–6

"Behold, the days are coming, declares the LORD, when I will raise up for David a righteous Branch, and he shall reign as king and deal wisely, and shall execute justice and righteousness in the land. In his days Judah will be saved, and Israel will dwell securely. And this is the name by which he will be called: 'The LORD is our righteousness.'"

❖ HYMNS

"Jesus, My Only Hope"
"White as Snow"

UNFAITHFULNESS

✦ CALL TO CONFESSION: JEREMIAH 3:6–10; COLOSSIANS 3:5–6

The Lord said to me in the days of King Josiah: "Have you seen what she did, that faithless one, Israel, how she went up on every high hill and under every green tree, and there played the whore? And I thought, 'After she has done all this she will return to me,' but she did not return, and her treacherous sister Judah saw it. She saw that for all the adulteries of that faithless one, Israel, I had sent her away with a decree of divorce. Yet her treacherous sister Judah did not fear, but she too went and played the whore. Because she took her whoredom lightly, she polluted the land, committing adultery with stone and tree. Yet for all this her treacherous sister Judah did not return to me with her whole heart, but in pretense, declares the Lord."

Put to death therefore what is earthly in you: sexual immorality, impurity, passion, evil desire, and covetousness, which is idolatry. On account of these the wrath of God is coming.

✦ PRAYER OF CONFESSION

Patient and loving Father,

You have been faithful to us in all things, keeping your promises to those who belong to you throughout all generations. But, Lord, we are not faithful to you. We have often struck you with our wayward wills, when our souls and bodies should embrace you with joy, gratitude, and love. Each new day exposes new corruptions in our hearts that we failed to see before, and each day we add to the long list of our offenses against you. Not only do we sin against your law, which we cannot keep, but we violate your love repeatedly, disobeying you even though we have drunk deeply from the fountain of your grace and mercy. We struggle to be faithful friends, spouses, siblings, parents, and children. We confess that our selfishness invades all of our relationships. Father, forgive us.

Lord, we have no merit before you; let the merit of Jesus stand for us. We are undeserving of your love, but he has earned your favor and affection for us. We are full of sin, but he is full of grace on our behalf. We disobey time and time again, but he obeyed every time, perfectly, in our place. All the powers of our bodies and souls are corrupted, but he remained pure and unblemished as he lived and died for us. We are unfaithful to you, but he was faithful for us. We thank you that you have chosen to look upon his goodness and pardon all our sins. Father, thank you.

Holy Spirit, show us more of Christ and change us into his likeness. Make us steadfast in our love for him and faithful in obedience. Let our weakness and indwelling sin humble us and fashion in our hearts a desperate desire for the help and hope that is found in him alone. May your deep love and mercy cause us to turn to you, to love you, to trust you, and to grow in faithfulness to you. Touch our sinful lips and fill them with praises for you, for you are gracious, and you alone can make our spirits right and true. Amen.

✤ ASSURANCE OF PARDON: JEREMIAH 32:37-41; 2 TIMOTHY 2:10-13

"Behold, I will gather them from all the countries to which I drove them in my anger and my wrath and in great indignation. I will bring them back to this place, and I will make them dwell in safety. And they shall be my people, and I will be their God. I will give them one heart and one way, that they may fear me forever, for their own good and the good of their children after them. I will make with them an everlasting covenant, that I will not turn away from doing good to them. And I will put the fear of me in their hearts, that they may not turn from me. I will rejoice in doing them good, and I will plant them in this land in faithfulness, with all my heart and all my soul."

Therefore I endure everything for the sake of the elect, that they also may obtain the salvation that is in Christ Jesus with eternal glory. The saying is trustworthy, for:

If we have died with him, we will also live with him;
if we endure, we will also reign with him;
if we deny him, he also will deny us;
if we are faithless, he remains faithful—

for he cannot deny himself.

✣ HYMNS

"God, Be Merciful to Me"
"How Deep the Father's Love"

THE FAITHFUL
SHEPHERD

❖ **CALL TO CONFESSION: JEREMIAH 3:12, 14–15**

"Return, faithless Israel,
> declares the LORD.
I will not look on you in anger,
> for I am merciful,
> > declares the LORD;
I will not be angry forever.

. . . .

Return, O faithless children,
> > declares the LORD;
> for I am your master;
I will take you, one from a city and two from a family,
> and I will bring you to Zion.

"And I will give you shepherds after my own heart, who will feed you with knowledge and understanding."

❖ **PRAYER OF CONFESSION**

Heavenly Father,

You are a kind and loving Shepherd. When we wander away from you, you bring us back. When we fall into sin, you restore us. When we are wounded, you heal us; and when we faint, you revive us. You protect us and lead us into green pastures, working all things for our good. You have given us your precious Son, and you never tire of forgiving us, loving us, and rescuing us. Father, thank you for your faithfulness and love for us in Christ.

Jesus, thank you for coming to earth to be the perfect Shepherd of your people. Your kind and patient care for foolish sheep melts our hearts with gratitude, and your compassion toward our many ongoing struggles with sin gives us hope. Thank you for laying down your life for us as our perfect sacrifice. You bore the heavy load of all our sin, and you dress us up in the shining robes of your perfect righteousness. Now you stand in heaven, our great Shepherd King, interceding for us and loving us. We could never deserve such faithful love and care, and we thank you.

Holy Spirit, you know our hearts. We are prone to wander away daily, and we need your help to live as shepherds and sheep in your church. Help our shepherds to lead wisely and to live lives of confession and repentance before us. Give them the courage to be humble, discerning, and loving. Give them strength to keep pursuing all kinds of weak and foolish sheep. Help those of us who are sheep to grow in grace and to respect our leaders well. Let us neither exalt them and treat them like heroes nor demean and discount them. May we honor them, giving thanks for your rich gift of gentle shepherds who feed us well from your Word every week. Make us a delight to them, and remind us to pray for them often. Make us good followers as we journey together to our heavenly home, where we will fall before our great Shepherd King and join the heavenly anthem of praise and adoration for the Lamb who was slain for us. In his great name we pray, amen.

✤ ASSURANCE OF PARDON: REVELATION 7:9–10, 14, 17

After this I looked, and behold, a great multitude that no one could number, from every nation, from all tribes and peoples and languages, standing before the throne and before the Lamb, clothed in white robes, with palm branches in their hands, and crying out with a loud voice, "Salvation belongs to our God who sits on the throne, and to the Lamb!" . . .

. . . "These are the ones [who] . . . have washed their robes and made them white in the blood of the Lamb. . . .

". . . The Lamb . . . will be their shepherd,
     and he will guide them to springs of living water,
and God will wipe away every tear from their eyes."

✤ HYMNS

"Ah, Holy Jesus"
"Wonderful, Merciful Savior"

PURITY

"For thus says the LORD of hosts, the God of Israel: Behold, I will silence in this place, before your eyes and in your days, the voice of mirth and the voice of gladness, the voice of the bridegroom and the voice of the bride.

"And when you tell this people all these words, and they say to you, 'Why has the LORD pronounced all this great evil against us? What is our iniquity? What is the sin that we have committed against the LORD our God?' then you shall say to them: 'Because your fathers have forsaken me, declares the LORD, and have gone after other gods and have served and worshiped them, and have forsaken me and have not kept my law, and because you have done worse than your fathers, for behold, every one of you follows his stubborn, evil will, refusing to listen to me.'"

✤ PRAYER OF CONFESSION

Heavenly Father,

You have given us a new name and a new righteousness that we could never have earned. You delight in us and rejoice over us like a captivated bridegroom, and we can barely comprehend your great love for rebels like us. We confess that we should rejoice over you with all our hearts, all day, every day; and yet we find our hearts and minds full of many other things. We allow our sexuality to define and ensnare us instead of marveling at such a great gift and all that it teaches us about your burning love for us. Father, forgive us for our lust, selfish fantasies, and overt acts of sexual sin. Forgive us for our cold rejection of sexuality for sinful reasons, as though it were dirty and we too pure to see its beauty. Lord, have mercy on us.

Lord Jesus, we thank you for your life of perfect purity on our behalf. You didn't let your mind wander into sinful sexual imaginings or use men and women for your own selfish desires. You burned with holy love for your Father, even as you ate with prostitutes and tax collectors, loving and forgiving them with a tender heart. Jesus, we don't feel like a prize worth winning, yet you counted it a joy to endure the cross for us. Thank you.

Holy Spirit, we live in a world full of temptation and have a strong enemy who assaults us. Our own hearts and desires give us trouble, and we need you to be at work in us. Change our hearts to love what you love and to desire your will more than our own. When we long for love and you do not give it as we wish, help us to trust you and run to you, believing that you are always for us. When we sin, turn our eyes to Jesus and let us see ourselves covered in the gleaming robes of his righteousness and the dazzling jewels of our bridal headdress. Help us to hate our sin and love our Savior, throwing ourselves into his loving arms when we feel dirty, ashamed, and unlovable. Remind us often that though this world is a place of sin and suffering, we are on our way to the greatest wedding of all time. On that day, we will see the lover of our souls face to face and will fall at his feet, completely lost in wonder at his love for us while we were yet sinners. Amen.

✤ ASSURANCE OF PARDON: ISAIAH 61:10–11

> I will greatly rejoice in the LORD;
>> my soul shall exult in my God,
> for he has clothed me with the garments of salvation;
>> he has covered me with the robe of righteousness,
> as a bridegroom decks himself like a priest with a beautiful headdress,
>> and as a bride adorns herself with her jewels.
> For as the earth brings forth its sprouts,
>> and as a garden causes what is sown in it to sprout up,
> so the Lord GOD will cause righteousness and praise
>> to sprout up before all the nations.

✤ HYMNS

"Beneath the Cross of Jesus"
"Jesus, Lover of My Soul"
"Jesus! What a Friend for Sinners!"

BEAUTY (1)

✤ CALL TO CONFESSION: EZEKIEL 16:8–15

"When I passed by you again and saw you, behold, you were at the age for love, and I spread the corner of my garment over you and covered your nakedness; I made my vow to you and entered into a covenant with you, declares the Lord GOD, and you became mine. Then I bathed you with water and washed off your blood from you and anointed you with oil. I clothed you also with embroidered cloth and shod you with fine leather. I wrapped you in fine linen and covered you with silk. And I adorned you with ornaments and put bracelets on your wrists and a chain on your neck. And I put a ring on your nose and earrings in your ears and a beautiful crown on your head. Thus you were adorned with gold and silver, and your clothing was of fine linen and silk and embroidered cloth. You ate fine flour and honey and oil. You grew exceedingly beautiful and advanced to royalty. And your renown went forth among the nations because of your beauty, for it was perfect through the splendor that I had bestowed on you, declares the Lord GOD.

"But you trusted in your beauty and played the whore because of your renown and lavished your whorings on any passerby; your beauty became his."

✤ PRAYER OF CONFESSION

Heavenly Father,

We confess to you that we are far more captivated by our idols than we are by you. Even though you have rescued us at great cost to yourself, we rebel against your deep love every day. We nurture many secret, sinful desires, even while appearing outwardly obedient. Even when you bless us with strong desires to obey, our flesh is weak and habitually distracted by beauty that we can see, feel, and touch. We are devoted to the pursuit of other lovers who make us feel valuable, powerful, safe, desirable, important, and worthy. You have every right to call us to faithfulness in all matters of love and sexuality, yet we rebel against you and give our beauty to other lovers time and time again. You have given us romantic love and sexual delight as pure gifts, but we sell our souls for cheap imitations that leave us feeling sick and empty. Father, forgive us for our adulterous hearts.

Lord Jesus, in your earthly life, you did not surround yourself with beautiful people. You lovingly pursued those who were disfigured with illness and crippled by sin and misery. You touched outcasts and embraced the most unlovely members of society. You forgave notorious sexual sinners and welcomed them. Though you walked this earth in a weak human body, you did not allow love to awaken sinfully in your heart or misuse sexuality to gratify yourself. In moments of great temptation you remained sexually pure and obedient, knowing that we would need your righteousness in order to stand in our day of trouble. Now you lavish us with the beauty and splendor of your holiness in spite of our remaining sin. Jesus, thank you for being beautiful on our behalf and for making us like you.

Holy Spirit, help us not to trust in our own beauty or to be dazzled by the alluring power of sexual temptation. Instead, help us to see the ravishing beauty of our Savior: the scars that still mark him, his glorious head crowned with thorns, his blood flowing freely from the wound in his side. Melt our stony hearts with his tender love and faithful obedience, until our other lovers lie silenced in the dust. When we fall into sin and are tempted to spiral into shame and despair, show us Christ again. May the depths of our sin daily reveal the heights of his love and his great power to save us. Wean our souls from the trinkets we dabble with, and cause us to long for Christ above all things. Satisfy our souls with him, and make him dear and precious to us. May he become our purest pleasure, and his love the delightful playground of our souls. In his name we pray, amen.

✤ ASSURANCE OF PARDON: ISAIAH 53:1–5

Who has believed what he has heard from us?
　　And to whom has the arm of the LORD been revealed?
For he grew up before him like a young plant,
　　and like a root out of dry ground;

✤ 103 ✤

he had no form or majesty that we should look at him,
   and no beauty that we should desire him.
He was despised and rejected by men,
   a man of sorrows and acquainted with grief;
and as one from whom men hide their faces
   he was despised, and we esteemed him not.

Surely he has borne our griefs
   and carried our sorrows;
yet we esteemed him stricken,
   smitten by God, and afflicted.
But he was pierced for our transgressions;
   he was crushed for our iniquities;
upon him was the chastisement that brought us peace,
   and with his wounds we are healed.

✤ HYMNS

"Carried to the Table"
"He Was Wounded for Our Transgressions"

SHEPHERDS
AND SHEEP

"Thus says the Lord GOD: Ah, shepherds of Israel who have been feeding yourselves! Should not shepherds feed the sheep? You eat the fat, you clothe yourselves with the wool, you slaughter the fat ones, but you do not feed the sheep. The weak you have not strengthened, the sick you have not healed, the injured you have not bound up, the strayed you have not brought back, the lost you have not sought, and with force and harshness you have ruled them. So they were scattered, because there was no shepherd, and they became food for all the wild beasts. My sheep were scattered; they wandered over all the mountains and on every high hill. My sheep were scattered over all the face of the earth, with none to search or seek for them."

✤✤✤

When [Jesus] went ashore he saw a great crowd, and he had compassion on them, because they were like sheep without a shepherd. And he began to teach them many things.

✤✤✤

"I am the good shepherd. The good shepherd lays down his life for the sheep. . . . I am the good shepherd. I know my own and my own know me."

✤ PRAYER OF CONFESSION

Almighty God,

Praise is due to you from all your creatures, for your works display your attributes and fulfill all your designs. You are the King of Kings, and at your will, empires rise and fall; you sit above the circle of the earth and govern all things according to your will and for your glory. Yet you are also a kind and loving Shepherd, carrying us in your heart and gently leading us through green pastures and painful valleys. You are powerful and full of compassion for your weak sheep, and we thank you for stooping to care for us with tenderness.

We are a small flock of your people, and as you call us to live together in peace, we know that we will fall short of your commands. Those of us who are called to lead will be tempted to seek power and use it for our own benefit, and to rule with a heavy hand. Lord, give compassion, gentleness, humility, and sacrificial love to those who you call to leadership in your church. Thank you for the perfect leadership of Jesus Christ, which covers and atones for each pastor, elder, and deacon. Give them courage to work hard and grace to fail, to learn, and to grow. Make them quick to repent when they sin, so they can lead us to the cross.

Those of us who are called to follow will be tempted to rebel and wander. We will be stubborn at times, and weak, and difficult to love. Thank you for the perfect submission of Jesus to his Father's will, which covers and protects us from ourselves. Make us humble, teachable, patient, and supportive toward those who are called to watch over our souls. Help us to confess our sin and repent quickly of it, so that we will be a delight to our leaders.

Holy Spirit, do not let pride swell up in our hearts. Humble us when we sin, and lead us to Christ. There, may we find the comfort of the gospel. We have a great advocate to calm our fears and a perfect Lamb who has died in our place. We have a reconciled Father, a powerful Shepherd, a compassionate friend, and a Savior who is willing and able to save us to the uttermost. In the name of the Chief Shepherd, we ask all these things, amen.

✤ ASSURANCE OF PARDON: 1 PETER 2:21–25

For to this you have been called, because Christ also suffered for you, leaving you an example, so that you might follow in his steps. He committed no sin, neither was deceit found in his mouth. When he was reviled, he did not revile in return; when he suffered, he did not threaten, but continued entrusting himself to him who judges justly. He himself bore our sins in his body on the tree, that we might die to sin and live to righteousness. By his wounds you have been healed. For you were straying like sheep, but have now returned to the Shepherd and Overseer of your souls.

✤ HYMNS

"Ah, Holy Jesus"
"Higher Throne"

SHAME

✤ CALL TO CONFESSION: DANIEL 9:7–11

"To you, O Lord, belongs righteousness, but to us open shame, as at this day, to the men of Judah, to the inhabitants of Jerusalem, and to all Israel, those who are near and those who are far away, in all the lands to which you have driven them, because of the treachery that they have committed against you. To us, O LORD, belongs open shame, to our kings, to our princes, and to our fathers, because we have sinned against you. To the Lord our God belong mercy and forgiveness, for we have rebelled against him and have not obeyed the voice of the LORD our God by walking in his laws, which he set before us by his servants the prophets. All Israel has transgressed your law and turned aside, refusing to obey your voice."

✤ PRAYER OF CONFESSION

Merciful heavenly Father,

We have all turned away and rebelled against you. Some of us have openly flouted your laws and publicly pursued pathways of disobedience. Others have outwardly conformed, but inside—in our hearts—have rejected your wisdom and treasured our idols. Our thoughts, our words, and our deeds are all stained with sin. We are not blameless or innocent in your sight or our own. Even our best deeds have often been done in order to justify ourselves and establish our own righteousness apart from you, because we refuse to rely on your grace and mercy. You have given us your perfect Word, and we have neglected and ignored its teaching, because we wanted to be free to pursue our own desires. We are desperate sinners who deserve to be cut off from you forever. Lord, remember your mercy and have compassion on us in our great weakness.

Jesus, thank you that you, the Righteous One, entered our sin-stained world and took on our flesh. You obeyed your Father and kept his laws perfectly, loving his Holy Word; then you gave us that righteousness and took into yourself our shame. At the cross, you were cut off from your Father, as we deserve to be. In your moment of great disgrace and reproach, you were not confounded or shaken. You remained faithful to your mission. When your Father hid his face and you experienced all of his overflowing anger poured out on you, you trusted in his everlasting love and compassion. You were driven away so that we could be gathered in as your beloved family. Because of you, we are now blameless and acceptable and welcomed in. Jesus, thank you for the luxurious gift of your obedience credited to us.

Holy Spirit, when we are fearful, give us the imagination of faith so that we can look forward and trust your promises. When shame overwhelms us, remind us that our shame did not overwhelm Christ, and that he destroyed it forever on the cross. Help us to remember your compassion toward us so we will come to you as weak and weary sinners, wounded by our fallenness, yet full of joy and hope in you. Give us hearts that genuinely desire to obey you and to love your law. Take our eyes off our own performance so that we may find deep comfort and confidence in the perfect obedience of our Savior. We pray in Jesus' glorious name, amen.

✦ ASSURANCE OF PARDON: ISAIAH 54:4–8

"Fear not, for you will not be ashamed;
  be not confounded, for you will not be disgraced;
for you will forget the shame of your youth,
  and the reproach of your widowhood you will remember
    no more.
For your Maker is your husband,
  the LORD of hosts is his name;
and the Holy One of Israel is your Redeemer,
  the God of the whole earth he is called.
For the LORD has called you
  like a wife deserted and grieved in spirit,
like a wife of youth when she is cast off,
  says your God.
For a brief moment I deserted you,
  but with great compassion I will gather you.

In overflowing anger for a moment
    I hid my face from you,
but with everlasting love I will have compassion on you,"
    says the Lord, your Redeemer.

✤ HYMNS

"I Come by the Blood"
"Not in Me"

WAITING (2)

✤ CALL TO CONFESSION: DANIEL 9:15–19

"And now, O Lord our God, who brought your people out of the land of Egypt with a mighty hand, and have made a name for yourself, as at this day, we have sinned, we have done wickedly.

"O Lord, according to all your righteous acts, let your anger and your wrath turn away from your city Jerusalem, your holy hill, because for our sins, and for the iniquities of our fathers, Jerusalem and your people have become a byword among all who are around us. Now therefore, O our God, listen to the prayer of your servant and to his pleas for mercy, and for your own sake, O Lord, make your face to shine upon your sanctuary, which is desolate. O my God, incline your ear and hear. Open your eyes and see our desolations, and the city that is called by your name. For we do not present our pleas before you because of our righteousness, but because of your great mercy. O Lord, hear; O Lord, forgive. O Lord, pay attention and act. Delay not, for your own sake, O my God, because your city and your people are called by your name."

✤ PRAYER OF CONFESSION

Heavenly Father,

We confess that, like little children, we hate to wait. We fuss and fret about our difficult circumstances until we are weary of crying, instead of resting in you and trusting your unmatched wisdom. We grasp for the things that our wisdom and appetites demand right now, rather than waiting patiently to receive the good gifts that you have planned for us in your perfect timing. Even good things regularly become the object of our over-desires. We persuade ourselves that we need riches, relationships, sex, children, food, or possessions to be happy and fulfilled, instead of recognizing your wisdom and perfect plan for our lives. You have given us exactly what we need, in perfect measure, with perfect love. Your Word exposes the perverse foolishness and ingratitude of our hearts.

Jesus, we desperately need to have the filthy, sin-stained rags of our wrong desires and over-desires removed, and our nakedness covered by your holy purity. While you lived among us, you always waited patiently for your Father's timing. You were never rushed or late, never out of step with the Holy Spirit's leading. You never pined for the things that your Father withheld from you, nor drew back when he handed you the cup of suffering. Clothe us in your holy purity and perfect patience, we pray.

Holy Spirit, renew our minds with your perfect holiness. Teach us how to wait patiently for the Father to answer us and how to endure without those things that we think we must have. Show us even how to survive our repeated failure and sin, by making Christ's beauty shine all the more clearly in the light of our own spiritual brokenness and ugliness. Grow within us daily a greater longing and eager expectation, as we await the day of Christ's appearing, when we will finally see him with our own eyes and all our purified desires will finally be fulfilled in him. Amen.

✠ ASSURANCE OF PARDON: 1 JOHN 1:7–9

But if we walk in the light, as he is in the light, we have fellowship with one another, and the blood of Jesus his Son cleanses us from all sin. If we say we have no sin, we deceive ourselves, and the truth is not in us. If we confess our sins, he is faithful and just to forgive us our sins and to cleanse us from all unrighteousness.

✠ HYMNS

"Out of the Depths"
"Thy Mercy, My God"

ADOPTION

✤ CALL TO CONFESSION: HOSEA 1:6–10

She conceived again and bore a daughter. And the LORD said to him, "Call her name No Mercy, for I will no more have mercy on the house of Israel, to forgive them at all. But I will have mercy on the house of Judah, and I will save them by the LORD their God. I will not save them by bow or by sword or by war or by horses or by horsemen."

When she had weaned No Mercy, she conceived and bore a son. And the LORD said, "Call his name Not My People, for you are not my people, and I am not your God."

Yet the number of the children of Israel shall be like the sand of the sea, which cannot be measured or numbered. And in the place where it was said to them, "You are not my people," it shall be said to them, "Children of the living God."

✤ PRAYER OF CONFESSION

Heavenly Father,

We admit to you the sad truth that we often live as if we were unpitied orphans. You have called us your sons and daughters and have made us alive in Christ; we ought to think about you and worship you all day long, and our hearts should constantly overflow with gratitude and obedience to you. Yet we find that we still are bent toward sin and drift easily away from you and toward temptation. We gratify the sinful desires of our bodies often, and in many different ways—through eating and drinking and sexual sins of many kinds. We medicate ourselves to escape our pain and entertain ourselves endlessly to distract our attention from our inner emptiness. Some of us control our bodies and submit them to rigorous physical, academic, and spiritual disciplines as a way of controlling our world and passions without you, trying to prove that if we work hard enough we can earn your pleasure. Father, forgive us for our many sins—those committed outwardly as well as those we cherish in secret.

Lord, thank you that although we still wrestle with sin, you have declared us righteous and given us the shining, perfect obedience of our Savior, Jesus Christ. He was the perfect Son who lived before you according to his true identity and mission, without ever faltering or falling. He hated sin and trusted the counsel of your will in all things, both when it was joyful and when it was dark and painful. He has earned every spiritual blessing for us, and his goodness surrounds, shields, and protects us each day. Father, thank you for Jesus.

Holy Spirit of the living God, you have begun a good work in us, and you will surely complete it. Though our sin may grieve you, it never stops you from working in us and through us. We thank you for the rich mercy that has saved us, raised us, and seated us with Christ. May thoughts of your immeasurable riches toward us in Christ, and the lavish provision that has been made for our sin, cheer our weary souls, strengthen us for obedience, and transform us more and more into the image of our sinless Savior. In his powerful name we pray, amen.

✤ ASSURANCE OF PARDON: 1 PETER 1:3–5

Blessed be the God and Father of our Lord Jesus Christ! According to his great mercy, he has caused us to be born again to a living hope through the resurrection of Jesus Christ from the dead, to an inheritance that is imperishable, undefiled, and unfading, kept in heaven for you, who by God's power are being guarded through faith for a salvation ready to be revealed in the last time. In this you rejoice.

✤ HYMNS

"Poor Sinner Dejected with Fear"
"Wonderful, Merciful Savior"

HARD HEARTS

✤ CALL TO CONFESSION: HOSEA 10:12

Sow for yourselves righteousness;
  reap steadfast love;
  break up your fallow ground,
for it is the time to seek the LORD,
  that he may come and rain righteousness upon you.

✤ PRAYER OF CONFESSION

Father of mercy,

We confess before you that our chief problem is not the sin of our hands and lips, but the hardness of our hearts. Though we love you and have tasted deeply of your mercy, our hearts are often cold and stony—slow to bear fruit for you. Our many sins come from the overflow of hearts that frequently feel dead toward you, and sometimes even full of fiery anger and cold rage. We cannot change our hearts, Lord. We are unable to make ourselves into a beautiful garden that produces righteousness and praise. Although we are no match for the depravity that we find in ourselves, we praise you that our hearts are never beyond your power to change and rescue. Father, thank you for your mercy and love.

Jesus, thank you that your heart was constantly soft and receptive to your Father's Word. That Word took root in the good soil of your life and bore abundant fruit of humility, service, self-sacrifice, and worship. Satan's temptations found no place to germinate in your life; you were indeed perfect as your heavenly Father is perfect. Thank you that your perfect life was not just an example that condemns our ugliness by its beauty. Thank you that it was for us, and that now, when your Father looks at us, he sees the fruitful soil of your life, not the rocky and barren wilderness of ours.

Holy Spirit, break up the fallow ground in our lives. Plow us with the difficulties and sufferings that we need; crush the boulders of our stubborn resistance to you; fertilize us with thoughts of the sweetness of the gospel; graft us firmly into the true vine, Jesus Christ; prune our wayward branches, so that our lives too might sprout up with righteousness and praise. Thank you that on that last day, our blind eyes will finally see clearly. Help us to long for the day when our hard and stony hearts will be fully melted and broken up, replaced with hearts of flesh, so that we shall bear fruit for you for all eternity. Amen.

✤ ASSURANCE OF PARDON: ISAIAH 55:9–11; 2 CORINTHIANS 9:9–10

"For as the heavens are higher than the earth,
   so are my ways higher than your ways
   and my thoughts than your thoughts.

"For as the rain and the snow come down from heaven
   and do not return there but water the earth,
making it bring forth and sprout,
   giving seed to the sower and bread to the eater,
so shall my word be that goes out from my mouth;
   it shall not return to me empty,
but it shall accomplish that which I purpose,
   and shall succeed in the thing for which I sent it."

✤✤✤

As it is written,

"He has distributed freely, he has given to the poor;
   his righteousness endures forever."

He who supplies seed to the sower and bread for food will supply and multiply your seed for sowing and increase the harvest of your righteousness.

✤ HYMNS

"All I Have Is Christ"
"Jesus Paid It All"
"Thy Mercy, My God"

ANGER

✠ CALL TO CONFESSION: JONAH 4:2–4; MATTHEW 5:44–46

"I knew that you are a gracious God and merciful, slow to anger and abounding in steadfast love, and relenting from disaster. Therefore now, O LORD, please take my life from me, for it is better for me to die than to live." And the LORD said, "Do you do well to be angry?"

[Jesus said] "But I say to you, Love your enemies and pray for those who persecute you, so that you may be sons of your Father who is in heaven. For he makes his sun rise on the evil and on the good, and sends rain on the just and on the unjust. For if you love those who love you, what reward do you have?"

✠ PRAYER OF CONFESSION

Glorious King and loving Father,

Your forgiveness and compassion far exceed our wildest dreams, but we are angry, resentful, and confused sinners. At times, our lips are ready to confess, but our hearts are slow to feel and our ways reluctant to change. Unmask our sin's deformity until we hate it and turn away from it instead of turning away from you. Like Jonah, we are often angry with you when people whom we dislike or hate seem to prosper and get away with evil. Instead of running to you for relief from our sin, we run from you, rehearsing the sins of others in our minds and feeling superior to them. We want you to be patient and merciful toward us when we sin against you many times each day, but we want those who sin against us to suffer and pay for their sin. Sometimes we don't even know that we're angry with you. Instead of hot tempers and furious rage, we indulge in cold disdain and apparent indifference, taking pride in our self-control while we nurture bitter and judgmental thoughts. Father, we all struggle with unrighteous, selfish anger and are worthy of your wrath against our sin. Lord, have mercy on us and forgive us for our profound hypocrisy, for while we were still your enemies, you gave your Son for us.

Spotless Lamb of God, you willingly stood condemned in our place and sealed our pardon with your blood. Thank you for your obedience and death, which have purchased our salvation. Thank you for praying for your enemies, even while they scoffed at you, whipped you, and nailed you to a cross. Thank you for bearing your Father's anger without becoming angry, and for yielding patiently to your Father's will when he didn't answer your prayer, giving you the bitter cup to drink for us. Thank you for choosing to die out of love for your people. Thank you for giving your record of perfect, loving forgiveness to us as a free and priceless gift. We stand in your love and power alone and are grateful.

Holy Spirit, help us to see our anger toward you. Remove our blindness; give us the courage to confess our rage, the grace to repent of it, and the faith to find comfort and joy in your forgiveness. Give us godly sorrow for our sin, and help us to cry out for mercy and pardon. Work in each of us a deeper, stronger faith that is powerful and confident in the cross. Give us soft and tender tears of repentance so that we see the glory of the cross more brightly. Help us to rest and rejoice in the wounds that have paid all of our debt, and give us hearts that are filled with awe at your amazing love for ruined sinners like us. Help us to frolic joyfully in the gushing torrent of your forgiveness and love, until streams of mercy flow sweetly from us toward sinners all around us. In the saving name of Jesus Christ we pray, amen.

✤ ASSURANCE OF PARDON: MICAH 7:18–20

Who is a God like you, pardoning iniquity
   and passing over transgression
   for the remnant of his inheritance?
He does not retain his anger forever,
   because he delights in steadfast love.
He will again have compassion on us;
   he will tread our iniquities underfoot.

You will cast all our sins
into the depths of the sea.

❖ HYMNS

"Come, Thou Fount of Every Blessing"
"In Christ Alone"

JUSTICE (1)

✤ CALL TO CONFESSION: MICAH 6:6–8

"With what shall I come before the LORD,
    and bow myself before God on high?
Shall I come before him with burnt offerings,
    with calves a year old?
Will the LORD be pleased with thousands of rams,
    with ten thousands of rivers of oil?
Shall I give my firstborn for my transgression,
    the fruit of my body for the sin of my soul?"
He has told you, O man, what is good;
    and what does the LORD require of you
but to do justice, and to love kindness,
    and to walk humbly with your God?

✤ PRAYER OF CONFESSION

Almighty and holy God,

Your love for justice delights our hearts. If you were not a just and holy God, this world, which you created and govern down to the most microscopic detail, would be unbearable to live in. However, we also admit that your love for justice terrifies our souls. If we were to count the sins that we have committed only today, we know that we would deserve your great anger and punishment. We have entertained evil thoughts toward others and have preferred ourselves and our favorite people over those who are outcasts in need of our love and care. We have made little of our sins, excusing them and even using your great forgiveness as a way of avoiding your commands. We have wearied you by laughing over evil things that we ought to hate. We have grieved you by hating good things and calling them evil, simply because they bore us or make us feel uncomfortable. Father, we deserve your judgment. Lord, have mercy on us.

We thank you that you have poured out the whole fire of your wrath on Jesus in our place. He never wearied you, but brought you perfect delight during every moment of his life. He hated evil and loved good, and he went out of his way to minister to those who were marginalized and unloved. We thank you that you are willing to look on his obedience and allow it to stand in our place. Father, thank you.

Holy Spirit, there is nothing we can do to satisfy God's justice. If even our best acts are like filthy rags, then we need the goodness of Jesus to cover us just as much on our best days as on our worst days. Remind us often that the blood of Christ erases our sin, and that God speaks to us in love, not in exasperation and disappointment. Ignite our hearts with a fiery gratitude that compels us to adore our Savior and to love what he calls good. Fill our hearts with your astonishing love, and send us out into a hurting world to love the fatherless, the widow, the strange, and the awkward, in the name of our Lord and Savior, Jesus Christ. Amen.

✤ ASSURANCE OF PARDON: ISAIAH 42:1-4; 1 PETER 2:21-24

Behold my servant, whom I uphold,
    my chosen, in whom my soul delights;
I have put my Spirit upon him;
    he will bring forth justice to the nations.
He will not cry aloud or lift up his voice,
    or make it heard in the street;
a bruised reed he will not break,
    and a faintly burning wick he will not quench;
    he will faithfully bring forth justice.
He will not grow faint or be discouraged
    till he has established justice in the earth;
    and the coastlands wait for his law.

✤✤✤

For to this you have been called, because Christ also suffered for you, leaving you an example, so that you might follow in his steps. He committed no sin, neither was deceit found in his mouth. When he was reviled, he did not revile in return; when he suffered, he did not threaten, but continued entrusting himself to him who judges justly. He himself bore our sins in his body on the tree, that we might die to sin and live to righteousness. By his wounds you have been healed.

✦ HYMNS

"Not in Me"
"The Son of God Came Down"

HONESTY

❖ CALL TO CONFESSION: MATTHEW 5:33–37;
PSALM 15:1–2, 5

"You have heard that it was said to those of old, 'You shall not swear falsely, but shall perform to the Lord what you have sworn.' But I say to you, Do not take an oath at all, either by heaven, for it is the throne of God, or by the earth, for it is his footstool, or by Jerusalem, for it is the city of the great King. And do not take an oath by your head, for you cannot make one hair white or black. Let what you say be simply 'Yes' or 'No'; anything more than this comes from evil."

O Lord, who shall sojourn in your tent?
Who shall dwell on your holy hill?

He who walks blamelessly and does what is right
and speaks truth in his heart;
. . . .
He who does these things shall never be moved.

❖ PRAYER OF CONFESSION

God of truth and revelation,

Make us humble disciples in the school of Christ. Teach us daily that we are fallen, sinful creatures who justly deserve everlasting destruction. We nurture lies, deep in our hearts. We distrust you and your promises, despite how clearly you have revealed yourself in history and in Scripture. We believe Satan's lie that you do not desire our good, our joy, or our happiness, and so we excuse our self-destructive pursuit of our own desires and our dismissal of your wise and loving instruction. We do not speak truthfully with one another, but we constantly spin, minimize, or excuse our sin while we inflate, exalt, and call attention to our selfishly motivated good works. We neglect your life-giving Word ourselves, and we weaponize your truth in order to accuse and control others. We despise others with whom we disagree, when everything that we have learned about you and your world is a gift of your Spirit.

Lord Jesus, thank you for not despising our ignorance from the enlightened glories of heaven. Thank you for taking on humanity in order to live among us. You proclaimed truth to us in order to call us from the kingdom of darkness into the kingdom of light. You lived a life of genuine truthfulness and integrity, lovingly confronting spiritual know-it-alls and comforting the spiritually downcast. You spoke truth with grace and gentleness, not to tear down but to bind up, and you pointed lie-captured hearts back to the reality of your Father's loving care.

Holy Spirit, lift the fog and darkness of our unbelief. Shine the light of your truth on our darkened minds. Show us Jesus Christ in all his beauty and loveliness, all his grace and compassion. Lead us daily to the cross, so that we may contemplate in his sufferings the immensity of his love for us. Holy Spirit, deepen in us an understanding of these profound truths, and do not let Satan deceive us with his cunning lies. In Jesus' name, amen.

❖ ASSURANCE OF PARDON: JOHN 1:14, 16–17; 14:6

The Word became flesh and dwelt among us, and we have seen his glory, glory as of the only Son from the Father, full of grace and truth. . . . For from his fullness we have all received, grace upon grace. For the law was given through Moses; grace and truth came through Jesus Christ.

Jesus said . . . , "I am the way, and the truth, and the life. No one comes to the Father except through me."

❖ HYMNS

"God, Be Merciful to Me"
"Speak, O Lord"

PRAYER

✤ CALL TO CONFESSION: MATTHEW 6:5–6

"And when you pray, you must not be like the hypocrites. For they love to stand and pray in the synagogues and at the street corners, that they may be seen by others. Truly, I say to you, they have received their reward. But when you pray, go into your room and shut the door and pray to your Father who is in secret. And your Father who sees in secret will reward you."

✤ PRAYER OF CONFESSION

Loving heavenly Father,

We may not remember to pray often, and yet we worry about prayer a great deal. We worry about how we sound when we pray and about who is listening. We think about how long we pray and are eager to check it off our list of duties when we are done. We doubt that you hear us or care about us enough to listen to our sorrows. We think that we have to clean ourselves up in order to pray, and we wonder if we disgust you with our sin and weakness. Father, forgive us.

Some of us love to pray. We want people to hear us and are eager to impress others with how spiritual we sound. We plan our public prayers carefully and are delighted when others notice our excellent prayers. In our hearts, we scoff at those who struggle to pray and don't do it very well. Father, forgive us.

Jesus, you prayed perfectly for us, and by your Spirit you make all of our prayers perfectly acceptable to our Father. As our great High Priest, you stand in heaven now, praying for your people and pleading for us. Jesus, thank you.

Holy Spirit, you pray on our behalf when we cannot pray, and you teach us to pray. Give us strong desires to come often to the throne of grace in order to receive help in our time of need. We need you many times, each and every day. Remind us to pray, and make us willing and able to cast all our cares on you, remembering that you care for us and are the only refuge for our weary and discouraged souls. In the name of Christ we pray, amen.

❖ ASSURANCE OF PARDON: PSALM 66:19–20; HEBREWS 10:19–23

But truly God has listened;
    he has attended to the voice of my prayer.

Blessed be God,
    because he has not rejected my prayer
    or removed his steadfast love from me!

Therefore, brothers, since we have confidence to enter the holy places by the blood of Jesus, by the new and living way that he opened for us through the curtain, that is, through his flesh, and since we have a great priest over the house of God, let us draw near with a true heart in full assurance of faith, with our hearts sprinkled clean from an evil conscience and our bodies washed with pure water. Let us hold fast the confession of our hope without wavering, for he who promised is faithful.

❖ HYMNS

"I Come by the Blood"
"Nothing That My Hands Can Do"

SEEKING GOD'S KINGDOM

✤ CALL TO CONFESSION: MATTHEW 6:9–13, 33

"Pray then like this:

> "Our Father in heaven,
> hallowed be your name.
> Your kingdom come,
> your will be done,
>   on earth as it is in heaven.
> Give us this day our daily bread,
> and forgive us our debts,
>   as we also have forgiven our debtors.
> And lead us not into temptation,
>   but deliver us from evil.
> [For yours is the kingdom and the power
>   and the glory, forever. Amen. . . .]*

". . . Seek first the kingdom of God and his righteousness, and all these things will be added to you."

✤ PRAYER OF CONFESSION

Heavenly Father,

We confess with our lips the blessedness of seeking your kingdom first, but our lives proclaim a different story. We sing the wonders of your love, but we grumble and complain when our desires are not fulfilled. We say that we follow a loving God who does what is best for us, but often we want to be our own gods, running the world in our own way. We declare that we long for the coming of your kingdom, but often we are more interested in the gifts that you give us than we are in you.

---

* These two lines are not found in some of the most ancient manuscripts.

Instead of following you, we are prone to follow our wisdom, our desires, and our own kingdoms. Father, forgive us for this prideful selfishness.

Lord Jesus, thank you that you are the King who reigns in truth and love. You showed us this love by becoming one of us and following your Father's will in our place. When Satan tempted you with the glory and power of your own kingdom, you rebuked him and followed the path of suffering instead. You laid down your life so that we could flourish in your kingdom forever. Thank you for this disarming kindness and love.

Holy Spirit, grow in us the desire to follow you, because we are still sinful, blind, and easily distracted. Help us to see the glory of your kingdom and to love it more than we love our own. Delight our hearts with your goodness until we bow our will to you joyfully. Give us grace to stand in obedience, knowing that without you we can do nothing. Give us grace to run to you when we fall, knowing that in Christ we have all the righteousness we will ever need. Help us to trust that your will is always done on this earth, even when it looks like Satan is winning. Help us to die to ourselves and to serve your kingdom with humble gratitude, boasting in the sweet name of our Savior, Jesus Christ. Amen.

✤ ASSURANCE OF PARDON: COLOSSIANS 1:10–14

Walk in a manner worthy of the Lord, fully pleasing to him: bearing fruit in every good work and increasing in the knowledge of God; being strengthened with all power, according to his glorious might, for all endurance and patience with joy; giving thanks to the Father, who has qualified you to share in the inheritance of the saints in light. He has delivered us from the domain of darkness and transferred us to the kingdom of his beloved Son, in whom we have redemption, the forgiveness of sins.

✤ HYMNS

"Before the Throne of God Above"
"How Sweet the Name of Jesus Sounds"

THE ROCK

"Everyone then who hears these words of mine and does them will be like a wise man who built his house on the rock. And the rain fell, and the floods came, and the winds blew and beat on that house, but it did not fall, because it had been founded on the rock. And everyone who hears these words of mine and does not do them will be like a foolish man who built his house on the sand. And the rain fell, and the floods came, and the winds blew and beat against that house, and it fell, and great was the fall of it."

✤ PRAYER OF CONFESSION

Heavenly Father,

We know that you love us and care for us with perfect strength, love, and commitment, but we find it hard to trust in you for our spiritual, physical, and emotional safety. We try to earn your love through our own works and obedience instead of resting in the finished work of Christ. We protect ourselves from physical danger and can't trust you well when we are sick and our health and strength are threatened. We guard ourselves emotionally from others—we hide and escape instead of living openly and honestly. We deceive others when we are ashamed or scared; we manipulate others when we want things but can't speak openly. When they won't give us what we want, we bully others into doing our will. O God, forgive us for our weakness and sin.

Jesus, we are very weak, but you were strong for us. Thank you for loving others well and for trusting in your Father's strength and deliverance, even when it looked as though you were completely forsaken. Your perfect confidence in God led you to joyful worship of your Father; now we are given that beautiful perfection, and we are so grateful.

Holy Spirit, give us grace to trust and rest. Remind us often of our perfect safety in Christ; draw our eyes away from our fear and self-salvation strategies so that we may worship and adore Christ. May our confidence in him help us to move toward one another, and into a scary world, with love and self-sacrifice instead of self-defense. Fill us each day with outrageous, joyful gratitude that enables us to hide confidently within his grace and love. We pray in Jesus' name, amen.

✤ ASSURANCE OF PARDON: PSALM 61:2–4; 27:4–5

Lead me to the rock
   that is higher than I,
for you have been my refuge,
   a strong tower against the enemy.

Let me dwell in your tent forever!
   Let me take refuge under the shelter of your wings!

✤✤✤

One thing have I asked of the Lord,
   that will I seek after:
that I may dwell in the house of the Lord
   all the days of my life,
to gaze upon the beauty of the Lord
   and to inquire in his temple.

For he will hide me in his shelter
   in the day of trouble;
he will conceal me under the cover of his tent;
   he will lift me high upon a rock.

✤ HYMNS

"Cornerstone"
"Not What My Hands Have Done"

RELENTLESS LOVE

✤ CALL TO CONFESSION: MATTHEW 8:24–27

And behold, there arose a great storm on the sea, so that the boat was being swamped by the waves; but he was asleep. And they went and woke him, saying, "Save us, Lord; we are perishing." And he said to them, "Why are you afraid, O you of little faith?" Then he rose and rebuked the winds and the sea, and there was a great calm. And the men marveled, saying, "What sort of man is this, that even winds and sea obey him?"

✤ PRAYER OF CONFESSION

Loving heavenly Father,

Your love for us is relentless and unstoppable. We thank you that our remaining sin cannot shock you or cause you to reject us or abandon us, even though we continue to sin against you day after day. We confess that while our minds understand your great power, sovereignty, and love, and while our lips claim to trust you, we are easily undone by very small trials and difficulties. Mere trifles cast us into despair and anxiety, and we behave as though you don't care and will not protect, defend, and provide for us. We are silly creatures who run from you, even though you have always been faithful to your promise to walk with us through all the fiery trials to which you call us. Father, forgive us for our lack of faith, our pretentious prayers, our willful disobedience, and our blind and flagrant idolatry.

Jesus, thank you for obeying the will of your Father when he asked you to walk into the heart of the storm for us. Even though you wrestled with the temptation to run away, you willingly accepted the cup of God's wrath and endured the wild tempest of his just anger and indignation toward all our sin. We can scarcely believe that you would do that for us. Thank you for your glowing obedience, which covers and protects us even though we continue to run from you over and over again. Thank you for standing firm so that we could be counted as perfectly faithful and obedient in spite of ourselves.

Holy Spirit, thank you for your ongoing work in our lives. You have begun a good work that we cannot impede with our foolishness, and we are grateful. Open our eyes to our sin, and point us to Christ as the only hope for our weakness and willful transgression. Melt us with the love and obedience of our Savior; cause us to run toward him and throw ourselves into his arms instead of running away and drowning ourselves in sinful escape strategies. Humble us with our inability and our great need for Christ, and teach us to walk in grateful dependence upon him all the days of our lives. Give us growing faith to see your hand at work in us each day, through the many storms of life. In Christ alone we pray, amen.

✜ ASSURANCE OF PARDON: ISAIAH 43:1-4

But now thus says the LORD,
    he who created you, O Jacob,
    he who formed you, O Israel:
"Fear not, for I have redeemed you;
    I have called you by name, you are mine.
When you pass through the waters, I will be with you;
    and through the rivers, they shall not overwhelm you;
when you walk through fire you shall not be burned,
    and the flame shall not consume you.
For I am the LORD your God,
    the Holy One of Israel, your Savior.
I give Egypt as your ransom,
    Cush and Seba in exchange for you.
Because you are precious in my eyes,
    and honored, and I love you,
I give men in return for you,
    peoples in exchange for your life."

✜ HYMNS

"In Christ Alone"
"Jesus Draw Me Ever Nearer"

FEAR (1)

✤ CALL TO CONFESSION: MATTHEW 10:28

"Do not fear those who kill the body but cannot kill the soul. Rather fear him who can destroy both soul and body in hell."

✤ PRAYER OF CONFESSION

Heavenly Father,

How easily we become fearful and distressed by our difficult circumstances when it appears that life is out of control! We fear those who have the power to kill our bodies, feeling anxious about terrorists, criminals, and many other dangers in this fallen world. We forget that they must answer to you and have no power to send us to hell. We even fear those who have the power to embarrass us—to make us feel uncomfortable or ashamed. We dread the disapproval of those whose good opinion we crave, or of those who have power over us and can thwart our dreams and desires. We quickly forget your awesome power to lift up and bring down people and nations. We don't remember that you govern every molecule in this universe, including every thought, word, and deed that occurs. As a result, we act as if our futures lay entirely within our own grasp or were at the disposal of those around us. Forgive us for our faithless fear and for its opposite: our self-confident pride.

Lord Jesus, thank you for your humble and constant trust in your Father. You feared no one on earth; instead, you feared the Lord with perfect reverence. When evil men did their worst, nailing you to a cross and killing your body, you still entrusted your soul to your Father's hands. You entered the hell of suffering for our sins, so that we would never have to fear that terrible fate. Thank you that your perpetual, confident faith is now counted to us, as if it were our own.

Holy Spirit, give us a fresh boldness to face each new day—a boldness that flows from believing in God's promises and trusting in God's sovereign power and goodness. Teach us the proper fear of the Lord that is the beginning of wisdom. Enable us to resist the constant pressure to conform to the values of this world, and draw us to pray whenever we face troubles or joys in life. Help us to walk alongside each other in difficult times, bearing one another's burdens and reminding each other of the certain outcome of the race that is set before us: a joyous welcome into our Father's arms. Amen.

✤ ASSURANCE OF PARDON: ACTS 2:23–24; HEBREWS 12:1–2

"This Jesus, delivered up according to the definite plan and foreknowledge of God, you crucified and killed by the hands of lawless men. God raised him up, loosing the pangs of death, because it was not possible for him to be held by it."

Therefore, since we are surrounded by so great a cloud of witnesses, let us also lay aside every weight, and sin which clings so closely, and let us run with endurance the race that is set before us, looking to Jesus, the founder and perfecter of our faith, who for the joy that was set before him endured the cross, despising the shame, and is seated at the right hand of the throne of God.

✤ HYMNS

"His Be the Victor's Name"
"Laden with Guilt and Full of Fears"

WORSHIP

✤ CALL TO CONFESSION: MATTHEW 15:7–9

[Jesus said to the Pharisees,] "You hypocrites! Well did Isaiah prophesy of you, when he said:

> "'This people honors me with their lips,
>   but their heart is far from me;
> in vain do they worship me,
>   teaching as doctrines the commandments of men.'"

✤ PRAYER OF CONFESSION

Merciful and mighty God,

We thank you for the great honor and privilege of joining with the angels and archangels who gather around your throne to worship you. You alone deserve all of our adoration and praise, and we thank you for giving us a glimpse of this heavenly worship service whenever we gather with your people. We ought to be filled with awestruck wonder that we belong to you, our only wise King. We confess to you that instead of being amazed by this, we have grown accustomed to this thought and are sometimes bored with the obligation to gather with your people for worship. We think that we are doing you a favor when we come to church, and we arrive with distracted minds and divided hearts. We joyfully give the best of our time, energy, effort, gifts, and wealth to our favorite idols and interests while grudgingly laying our leftovers before you—and then being proud of that second-rate offering. We would never say that we despise you, yet we are easily capable of finding worship to be dull and boring, and of resenting your command to gather together weekly. Lord, have mercy on us. We are deeply sinful and selfish children whose best acts of worship are blemished, deformed, and twisted with self-interest and pride.

We thank you for Jesus Christ. He is the spotless Lamb who became our perfect sacrifice. His death paid the debt for our mountains of apathy and disdain, and we are grateful. We thank you for his life of perfect obedience and flawless worship on our behalf. He loved, honored, worshiped, and obeyed you with all his heart, soul, mind, and strength, and now his record has replaced our own. In him we are counted as perfect worshipers, and we fall before you and praise you for this wonderful gift of his righteousness.

Holy Spirit, stir our cold and lazy hearts with gratitude. Open our eyes to see all that is ours in Christ, until we can't stop praising him. May the knowledge of what we deserve, and the reality of what we have received, melt our stony hearts with joy, fill our dull minds with unbearable delight, and adorn our lips with exuberant praise. Help us to grow as worshipers, until the day we join the angels dressed in festival robes and gather around your throne to honor you as your righteous children made perfect in Christ. In his strong name we pray, amen.

✤ ASSURANCE OF PARDON: HEBREWS 12:18–19, 22–24, 28–29

For you have not come to what may be touched, a blazing fire and darkness and gloom and a tempest and the sound of a trumpet and a voice whose words made the hearers beg that no further messages be spoken to them. . . . But you have come to Mount Zion and to the city of the living God, the heavenly Jerusalem, and to innumerable angels in festal gathering, and to the assembly of the firstborn who are enrolled in heaven, and to God, the judge of all, and to the spirits of the righteous made perfect, and to Jesus, the mediator of a new covenant, and to the sprinkled blood that speaks a better word than the blood of Abel. . . .

. . . Therefore let us be grateful for receiving a kingdom that cannot be shaken, and thus let us offer to God acceptable worship, with reverence and awe, for our God is a consuming fire.

✤ HYMNS

"He Is Jesus"
"How Sweet the Name of Jesus Sounds"
"Revelation Song"

THE RIGHTEOUS JUDGE

"When the Son of Man comes in his glory, and all the angels with him, then he will sit on his glorious throne. Before him will be gathered all the nations, and he will separate people one from another as a shepherd separates the sheep from the goats. And he will place the sheep on his right, but the goats on the left. Then the King will say to those on his right, 'Come, you who are blessed by my Father, inherit the kingdom prepared for you from the foundation of the world. For I was hungry and you gave me food, I was thirsty and you gave me drink, I was a stranger and you welcomed me, I was naked and you clothed me, I was sick and you visited me, I was in prison and you came to me.' Then the righteous will answer him, saying, 'Lord, when did we see you hungry and feed you, or thirsty and give you drink? And when did we see you a stranger and welcome you, or naked and clothe you? And when did we see you sick or in prison and visit you?' And the King will answer them, 'Truly, I say to you, as you did it to one of the least of these my brothers, you did it to me.'

"Then he will say to those on his left, 'Depart from me, you cursed, into the eternal fire prepared for the devil and his angels. For I was hungry and you gave me no food, I was thirsty and you gave me no drink, I was a stranger and you did not welcome me, naked and you did not clothe me, sick and in prison and you did not visit me.' Then they also will answer, saying, 'Lord, when did we see you hungry or thirsty or a stranger or naked or sick or in prison, and did not minister to you?' Then he will answer them, saying, 'Truly, I say to you, as you did not do it to one of the least of these, you did not do it to me.' And these will go away into eternal punishment, but the righteous into eternal life."

✠ PRAYER OF CONFESSION

Heavenly Father,

We thank you that you are a righteous judge. You define goodness and fairness in your universe, and we can trust you far more than we can ever trust our own sense of justice. We also thank you for your patience with us, which staggers our imaginations. Lord, we speak hard words against you in our hearts every day. If we examined every thought that flows through our minds, we would discover countless grumblings and accusations against you. We often serve you for many selfish reasons and think that you owe us what we want in exchange. We know this by the way that our hearts flare when we don't get what we want and, even worse, by our bitterness when others whom we think less deserving get exactly what we want. O God, have mercy on us and forgive us. If you were to give us what we truly deserve, we couldn't endure it for a moment.

We thank you for Jesus. You poured out on him the anger that we deserve, and he did endure it. He lived the perfect life, which earned your pleasure, and he paid the awful debt of all our sin. Our holy judge was judged in our place, and now we stand in his goodness with all the righteousness we need. Thank you for looking on his life and death, and for pardoning us.

Holy Spirit, we are weak and forgetful. Our minds are full of many things, and the drift of our thoughts is always away from you. We need your help in order to think clearly about Christ and remember him. We need you to melt our hard hearts with gratitude, for we cannot do that for ourselves. We need you to bring us to repentance, time and time again, when our souls rise up to grumble and accuse you of injustice. Humble us with the remembrance of Christ's unbelievable love and patience with us, and fill us with desire to worship and adore him. Amen.

❧ ASSURANCE OF PARDON: ACTS 10:38–43

"God anointed Jesus of Nazareth with the Holy Spirit and with power. He went about doing good and healing all who were oppressed by the devil, for God was with him. And we are witnesses of all that he did both in the country of the Jews and in Jerusalem. They put him to death by hanging him on a tree, but God raised him on the third day and made him to appear, not to all the people but to us who had been chosen by God as witnesses, who ate and drank with him after he rose from the dead. And he commanded us to preach to the people and to testify that he is the one appointed by God to be judge of the living and the dead. To him all the prophets bear witness that everyone who believes in him receives forgiveness of sins through his name."

✦ HYMNS

"Come, Thou Long-Expected Jesus"
"Joy to the World"

THE GOOD NEWS

✤ CALL TO CONFESSION: MATTHEW 28:18–20;
ROMANS 10:14–17

And Jesus came and said to them, "All authority in heaven and on earth has been given to me. Go therefore and make disciples of all nations, baptizing them in the name of the Father and of the Son and of the Holy Spirit, teaching them to observe all that I have commanded you. And behold, I am with you always, to the end of the age."

How then will they call on him in whom they have not believed? And how are they to believe in him of whom they have never heard? And how are they to hear without someone preaching? And how are they to preach unless they are sent? As it is written, "How beautiful are the feet of those who preach the good news!" But they have not all obeyed the gospel. For Isaiah says, "Lord, who has believed what he has heard from us?" So faith comes from hearing, and hearing through the word of Christ.

✤ PRAYER OF CONFESSION

God of our salvation,

What could we ever give to you in return for your greatest gift: your own dear Son? He is our peace and salvation, our Redeemer, our substitute. He stooped low to raise us up—was born like us that we might become like him. He united Deity and humanity, the Creator becoming created, so that one day we might shed our sinful flesh and be remade in his likeness. He worked out a perfect righteousness, which was given to us, so that we can draw near to you. When we cannot rise to him, he draws close and lifts us up to himself. He entered into holy war with Satan, defeating our enemy, winning our battle, and purchasing our eternal peace with you.

O God, these are tidings of great joy, and yet we often live without joy in our salvation. We find great joy in your good gifts without lifting our hearts to worship you, the giver of all good things. We prostitute our hearts daily; our attention and admiration are easily bought for a moment of pleasure and escape. We are relentless worshipers of ourselves—fearful of talking about you and appearing foolish, committed to our own agendas and brazenly unwilling to go wherever you would send us, captivated by our own little kingdoms instead of gratefully serving in yours. No wonder we are easily shaken when our eyes are always on ourselves and the fragile things in which we put our hope.

O God, have mercy on us. Though we desire to please you, we are weak and sinful, unable to stand in obedience unless you lift us up. Forgive us for the sin that remains in us. Though it frightens and troubles us, you have defeated it completely, giving us perfect peace in Christ. Thank you that we are forever united to him—his obedience is our very own, and your delight in him is always bathing us with your Fatherly pleasure.

Enlarge our hearts to celebrate this good news of great joy, for we are barely able to grasp the enormity of our salvation. Settle our hope and peace in the love of Christ, and make his throne the pleasure ground of our souls. Help us to love those around us, drawing them into your family by caring and speaking of your greatness in wise and loving ways, always ready to share the great news, and eager to explain the hope that is in us. Help us to sing of your goodness, loudly in our souls and joyfully when we are together, with hearts that are undone by your love and kindness to us. In Christ's great name we pray, amen.

✤ ASSURANCE OF PARDON: EPHESIANS 2:13–18

But now in Christ Jesus you who once were far off have been brought near by the blood of Christ. For he himself is our peace, who has made us both one and has broken down in his flesh the dividing wall of hostility by abolishing the law of commandments expressed in ordinances, that he might create in himself one new man in place of the two, so making peace, and might reconcile us both to God in one body through the cross, thereby killing the hostility. And he came and preached peace to you who were far off and peace to those who were near. For through him we both have access in one Spirit to the Father.

✤ HYMNS

"Poor Sinner Dejected with Fear"
"Hark! the Herald Angels Sing"

FEAR (2)

✤ CALL TO CONFESSION: MARK 4:35–38

On that day, when evening had come, he said to them, "Let us go across to the other side." And leaving the crowd, they took him with them in the boat, just as he was. And other boats were with him. And a great windstorm arose, and the waves were breaking into the boat, so that the boat was already filling. But he was in the stern, asleep on the cushion. And they woke him and said to him, "Teacher, do you not care that we are perishing?"

✤ PRAYER OF CONFESSION

Faithful Father,

We confess to you our fearful hearts and our fretful prayers. We look around us and see a world that feels dangerous and out of control. There are storms on all sides—waves that are ready to swamp our little boats and drown us and those whom we love. We easily forget that you are the Creator God who rules the wind and waves. We panic and accuse you of leaving us in danger, when all along your sovereign power is at work for good in our lives, even in the most painful and distressing circumstances. You hold in your hands our health, our money, our careers, our relationships, our children—everything that we have and everything that we are.

Lord Jesus, thank you for entering the storms of life with us. Thank you for enduring exhaustion, pain, sickness, broken relationships, and betrayal for us. The circumstances that so easily cause us to doubt God's love and care, you committed confidently into the hands of your sovereign Father. Thank you that you trusted perfectly in the darkest situations, in our place.

Holy Spirit, teach us to put our faith to work and to learn that we have a good and almighty Father who orchestrates our lives perfectly. Help us to be content in weakness, failure, suffering, and brokenness, recognizing that these gifts come to us from your hand. Through them, may we see more and more clearly our own weakness and inability, along with the fact that your grace is always sufficient for us. Amen.

✤ ASSURANCE OF PARDON: MARK 4:39–41

And he awoke and rebuked the wind and said to the sea, "Peace! Be still!" And the wind ceased, and there was a great calm. He said to them, "Why are you so afraid? Have you still no faith?" And they were filled with great fear and said to one another, "Who then is this, that even the wind and the sea obey him?"

✤ HYMNS

"Jesus, Priceless Treasure"
"None Other Lamb"

THE CHRIST

✤ CALL TO CONFESSION: LUKE 9:18–20

Now it happened that as he was praying alone, the disciples were with him. And he asked them, "Who do the crowds say that I am?" And they answered, "John the Baptist. But others say, Elijah, and others, that one of the prophets of old has risen." Then he said to them, "But who do you say that I am?" And Peter answered, "The Christ of God."

✤ PRAYER OF CONFESSION

Incomparable Savior,

We thank you, with all of our hearts, for your wondrous love in bearing all of our guilt on the cross. May your cross sweeten every bitterness in our lives, encourage us with hope in every trial, and connect us to you as the true vine—the only source of all our strength and power. Lord, we have died with you, are risen with you, and are seated with you already in heavenly places. Yet we find that sin continues to have great power over us, because we quickly forget who you are, and who we are in you. We are often self-absorbed—we struggle daily to deny ourselves and to choose obedience and love for others over pleasing ourselves. We wrestle with many sinful desires and with over-desires for many good things. When we do manage to serve others, we often take pride and pleasure in our own good conduct, and we use our serving to feel good about ourselves. Father, forgive us for the self-gratifying and self-exalting lives that we lead from moment to moment.

Jesus, thank you for giving up the praise and glory of heaven in order to please your Father and rescue us from ourselves. You denied yourself the adoration and worship that you richly deserved, in order to enter a world of people who would misunderstand, reject, and hate you. You lived a life of self-denial and sacrificial love for others, always obeying your Father, always putting the needs of others before your own. We thank you for your radiant robe of righteousness, which replaces the filthy and tattered rags of our attempts to be good. Although you are the anointed one of God, you paid the full price that we owed for sin at the cross, so that we could be freed from bondage to sin and death and from our relentless self-worship. Thank you.

Holy Spirit, we have been given a cross to carry before we wear the crown. We confess that self-love causes us to hate that cross and that human reason leads us to run from it. Without your help we cannot bear it. Spirit, remind us often that Jesus has carried that cross already for us, and that he will surely carry it with us from day to day. Increase our joy in the cross of Christ, and our wonder and admiration for all that was accomplished for us there, until our hearts melt and our self-worship gives way to profound delight in Jesus as our priceless treasure. As true worship fills the panorama of our souls, may we grow into people who swiftly turn away from our own desires in order to love others as we have been so greatly loved. We pray in the beautiful name of Jesus, amen.

✤ ASSURANCE OF PARDON: JOHN 14:1–6

"Let not your hearts be troubled. Believe in God; believe also in me. In my Father's house are many rooms. If it were not so, would I have told you that I go to prepare a place for you? And if I go and prepare a place for you, I will come again and will take you to myself, that where I am you may be also. And you know the way to where I am going." Thomas said to him, "Lord, we do not know where you are going. How can we know the way?" Jesus said to him, "I am the way, and the truth, and the life. No one comes to the Father except through me."

✤ HYMNS

"Jesus, Thy Blood and Righteousness"
"The Servant King"

REBELLIOUS PRODIGALS

✤ CALL TO CONFESSION: LUKE 18:9–14

He also told this parable to some who trusted in themselves that they were righteous, and treated others with contempt: "Two men went up into the temple to pray, one a Pharisee and the other a tax collector. The Pharisee, standing by himself, prayed thus: 'God, I thank you that I am not like other men, extortioners, unjust, adulterers, or even like this tax collector. I fast twice a week; I give tithes of all that I get.' But the tax collector, standing far off, would not even lift up his eyes to heaven, but beat his breast, saying, 'God, be merciful to me, a sinner!' I tell you, this man went down to his house justified, rather than the other. For everyone who exalts himself will be humbled, but the one who humbles himself will be exalted."

✤ PRAYER OF CONFESSION

Gracious heavenly Father,

Your name is love; in love, receive our prayers. Our sins are more than the sands of the sea, but where sin abounds your grace is even more abundant. Let us look to the cross of your beloved Son; let us view the preciousness of his atoning blood; let us listen to his never-failing intercession and whisper to our hearts, "Your sins are forgiven; be of good cheer; live in peace."

Father, we are often guilty of loving the gifts that you give us while rejecting you. We love the benefits of belonging to you, yet we do not cherish and nurture the greatest gift of all: our relationship with you as your adopted sons and daughters. Sometimes we rebel against you openly and angrily, breaking your laws and running far from you. At other times we rebel against you by carefully keeping your laws, as if by our obedience we could purchase your favor, love, and generosity. God, be merciful to us, for we are lost sinners. In both our rebellion and our obedience, we love ourselves far more than we love you. Father, forgive us.

Jesus, you have been the perfect son on our behalf. You loved your Father with all your heart and never failed to do his will with joy. You poured yourself out sacrificially for your brothers and sisters, giving up the privileges of sonship in order to bring us into your family and make us joint heirs with you. Jesus, thank you for seeking us, finding us, and giving us shining robes of your righteousness, with which we can stand before the Father.

Holy Spirit, humble us, we pray. We have nothing to bring to you in which we can boast. Melt our hearts when they are proud, cold, and full of self-righteousness. Reveal our sin to us so that we can repent. When we wander and rebel, draw us back time and time again to marvel at your endless patience and undying love. Comfort our hearts when they are shattered with the weight of indwelling sin, and revive our joy and hope in our faithful Savior and brother, Jesus Christ. Your grace gushes toward us like a mighty river from heaven; grant us still more grace, we pray! May our obedience flow back to you from hearts that are filled with gratitude and love. Let us cherish our loving heavenly Father far more than we love ourselves or the blessings of his generous gifts. We pray in Jesus' name, amen.

✤ ASSURANCE OF PARDON: GALATIANS 4:4–6

But when the fullness of time had come, God sent forth his Son, born of woman, born under the law, to redeem those who were under the law, so that we might receive adoption as sons. And because you are sons, God has sent the Spirit of his Son into our hearts, crying, "Abba! Father!"

✤ HYMNS

"Not in Me"
"The Son of God Came Down"

RESURRECTION

✤ CALL TO CONFESSION: JOHN 5:24–29

"Truly, truly, I say to you, whoever hears my word and believes him who sent me has eternal life. He does not come into judgment, but has passed from death to life.

"Truly, truly, I say to you, an hour is coming, and is now here, when the dead will hear the voice of the Son of God, and those who hear will live. For as the Father has life in himself, so he has granted the Son also to have life in himself. And he has given him authority to execute judgment, because he is the Son of Man. Do not marvel at this, for an hour is coming when all who are in the tombs will hear his voice and come out, those who have done good to the resurrection of life, and those who have done evil to the resurrection of judgment."

✤ PRAYER OF CONFESSION

Loving Father,

You know our inmost thoughts and the doubts that constantly shake us. With our lips we confess that we believe in the resurrection, but our persistent fears betray our unbelief. We say that in Christ we have everything we need for life and death, yet when our possessions, health, reputations, jobs, or families are threatened with loss or danger, we fret and fall apart. We know we will one day have new, glorious bodies, but we are quickly undone when our earthly bodies fail us. We run from discomfort and pain, and even withdraw from others who are suffering, unwilling to do the costly work of loving them well in their distress. Father, forgive our unbelief.

Jesus, you are the resurrection and the life. You entered this world of suffering and death, and gave yourself over into the hands of those who hated you and were determined to kill you. Yet, in your darkest moments, you fixed your eyes on the joy that was set before you: that after the resurrection you would possess us as your people forever. You never wavered in your desire to have us as your inheritance, or in your faith that the Father would accomplish this through your death and resurrection. Thank you for enduring through deep suffering in order that we may become like you and be with you forever.

Holy Spirit, you are the one who brings life to our dead souls, and will one day bring life back to these mortal bodies also. When we find ourselves in the depths of suffering and loss, enable us to cry out to you. When we labor hard and see no fruit, teach us to wait patiently for you, the God of the harvest. When we cannot believe well and we run to find comfort in our favorite earthly pleasures, strengthen our faith. Help our unbelief, and help us to survive the weakness of our flickering faith by resting in the perfection of Jesus on our behalf. In all of our trials and difficulties, fix our eyes on our heavenly inheritance, which is stored up for us in Christ in a place where no power in heaven, on earth, or under the earth can touch it. Come quickly, Lord Jesus! We long to be free from our sin and to enjoy you forever with sinless hearts, clear eyes, and minds devoted to knowing you and serving you with loving delight. Amen.

✤ ASSURANCE OF PARDON: 1 CORINTHIANS 15:20–26

But in fact Christ has been raised from the dead, the firstfruits of those who have fallen asleep. For as by a man came death, by a man has come also the resurrection of the dead. For as in Adam all die, so also in Christ shall all be made alive. But each in his own order: Christ the firstfruits, then at his coming those who belong to Christ. Then comes the end, when he delivers the kingdom to God the Father after destroying every rule and every authority and power. For he must reign until he has put all his enemies under his feet. The last enemy to be destroyed is death.

✤ HYMNS

"Before the Throne of God Above"
"Out of the Depths"

LOVE ONE ANOTHER (1)

✠ CALL TO CONFESSION: JOHN 13:34–35

"A new commandment I give to you, that you love one another: just as I have loved you, you also are to love one another. By this all people will know that you are my disciples, if you have love for one another."

✠ PRAYER OF CONFESSION

Loving heavenly Father,

Have mercy on us. Although we have all received your lavish love and unfailing forgiveness, we find it very hard to love each other well. Our fallen nature draws us to an endless fascination with ourselves, and to a strong tendency to despise people who are different from us or don't agree with us. We long to be praised and admired; when our desires are thwarted, we withdraw our affection from those who disappoint us and indulge ourselves with vicious, unkind thoughts toward them. Instead of cultivating a love that covers sin, we rehearse the sins of those whom we dislike in an effort to justify ourselves and feel superior. Father, forgive us, for we are broken and twisted lovers of ourselves. Thank you for discarding our sins, for burying them in the deepest sea, for refusing to remember our sin and hold it against us.

Lord Jesus, you volunteered to become a man and to allow the very creatures whom you made to sin against you in the deepest way. You lived a life of perfect goodness for us and loved others well, yet you were mocked, beaten, spat upon, and despised. In all of this, you prayed for the forgiveness of the ones who abused you most. Thank you for your obedience, which covers over our daily, petty dislike of others as well as our full-blown hatred toward those we despise. Without your death in our place and your righteousness credited to us, we could never enjoy the beaming delight of our heavenly Father. Thank you for meriting his pleasure for us, even though we are still very sinful.

Holy Spirit, we desperately need your help. Our minds wander into vicious thoughts before we even realize what is happening. Please show us when our thoughts are sinful, and help us to repent of them and accept the responsibility for them. Help us to run to the cross to be immersed in your forgiveness, love, and eternal welcome, so that we can love and forgive others with hearts that are melted with gratitude. Help us to capture sinful, unloving thoughts and to make them obedient to you, so that our behavior will be far more loving than the attitudes with which we frequently struggle. May the deep love of our Father, and the sacrificial love of our Savior, transform us from the inside out into people who respect, cherish, and readily forgive the most difficult people in our lives. We ask this in the name of Christ alone, and for the sake of his glory. Amen.

✤ ASSURANCE OF PARDON: 1 THESSALONIANS 3:11–13

Now may our God and Father himself, and our Lord Jesus, direct our way to you, and may the Lord make you increase and abound in love for one another and for all, as we do for you, so that he may establish your hearts blameless in holiness before our God and Father, at the coming of our Lord Jesus with all his saints.

✤ HYMNS

"A Debtor to Mercy"
"How Deep the Father's Love"

PEACE

✤ CALL TO CONFESSION: JOHN 16:33; COLOSSIANS 3:14–16

"I have said these things to you, that in me you may have peace. In the world you will have tribulation. But take heart; I have overcome the world."

Above all these put on love, which binds everything together in perfect harmony. And let the peace of Christ rule in your hearts, to which indeed you were called in one body. And be thankful. Let the word of Christ dwell in you richly, teaching and admonishing one another in all wisdom, singing psalms and hymns and spiritual songs, with thankfulness in your hearts to God.

✤ PRAYER OF CONFESSION

Heavenly Father,

Our hearts are constantly storm-tossed by our varied circumstances. When life is going well, we are elated and feel infinitely strong. When we face problems and frightening situations, we are cast down and feel sure that we will drown. Instead of thankfulness and peace, our hearts are often ruled by forgetfulness and fear. We imagine ourselves to be abandoned because of our sin and cut off. We feel isolated from one another as well as from you. We know that you have overcome this world, but our peace is fleeting and is built upon flimsy things, and we are not comforted by your strength and love. Father, forgive us.

Jesus, thank you for your perfect peace in all life's deepest trials. You were able to rest in the midst of the storm, because you knew that you were the Father's priceless treasure, whom he would not allow to see destruction. Even when the Father's wrath was poured out upon you for our sake, you rested in his sure promises and trusted in him. Thank you that this peace is now given to us as a free gift. Because of you, we are the Father's priceless treasure, his beloved children, whom he will never give up.

Holy Spirit, quiet our unruly hearts. Banish our fear and sadness with your truth. Give us the peace that we so often lack by reminding us of the rich word of Christ. Teach us to find solid hope in Christ's blood, which is shed for us. Thank you that even when nothing feels well with us, all is well with you—the gospel is true in spite of our feelings. Help us to celebrate this when our hearts are cold, our will is weak, and you do not remove our fear as we wish you would. May we encourage one another joyfully and boldly with this great news. In Jesus' name we pray, amen.

✤ ASSURANCE OF PARDON: EPHESIANS 2:11–22

Therefore remember that at one time you Gentiles in the flesh . . . were at that time separated from Christ, alienated from the commonwealth of Israel and strangers to the covenants of promise, having no hope and without God in the world. But now in Christ Jesus you who once were far off have been brought near by the blood of Christ. For he himself is our peace, who has made us both one and has broken down in his flesh the dividing wall of hostility by abolishing the law of commandments expressed in ordinances, that he might create in himself one new man in place of the two, so making peace, and might reconcile us both to God in one body through the cross, thereby killing the hostility. And he came and preached peace to you who were far off and peace to those who were near. For through him we both have access in one Spirit to the Father. So then you are no longer strangers and aliens, but you are fellow citizens with the saints and members of the household of God, built on the foundation of the apostles and prophets, Christ Jesus himself being the cornerstone, in whom the whole structure, being joined together, grows into a holy temple in the Lord. In him you also are being built together into a dwelling place for God by the Spirit.

✤ HYMNS

"In Christ Alone"
"Jesus, Priceless Treasure"
"It Is Well with My Soul"

THE GOSPEL

For I am not ashamed of the gospel, for it is the power of God for salvation to everyone who believes, to the Jew first and also to the Greek. For in it the righteousness of God is revealed from faith for faith, as it is written, "The righteous shall live by faith."

✤ PRAYER OF CONFESSION

Heavenly Father,

In the gospel, you have given us the rich treasure of forgiveness, life, and immortality. Yet we have been ashamed of that incredible gift and have often devalued and hidden it by our words and our actions. At times, we have publicly denied knowing you or having any acquaintance with Christianity, because we were embarrassed of other believers or afraid to suffer in any way for the sake of Christ. At other times, we have brought dishonor on that name when we have loudly proclaimed our faith and then spoken arrogantly or behaved rudely, judging and condemning those who wouldn't agree with us. We despise the gospel in our own thoughts when we believe that we really aren't too bad and can win your favor with a few more prayers and quiet times—a few good deeds and acts of penance. We mock the gospel when we live as though you love us more when we're good than when we struggle and fail, as though our best obedience could ever come close to the perfection you require. We often use "the gospel" as a slogan, instead of founding our lives upon it as a rock and a refuge. Father, forgive us.

Lord Jesus, thank you that the gospel is still true even when we are embarrassed by it, neglect it, and are bored by it. It remains your power at work for our salvation in spite of our ongoing weakness and sin. Thank you that our assurance is rooted in your perfect obedience throughout every moment of your life, and in your death and resurrection. You have won us and will hold us in your strong hands; you will never let us go. We will stand before you and live forever with you, and nothing can change that. We are undone by your kindness.

Holy Spirit, help us to guard the gospel well, for ourselves and for others. Teach us to treasure its truth in our own lives. When we sin against you repeatedly, remind us of the truth that we know, and help us to believe and experience its cleansing power. When others sin against us, help us to forgive them well for the gospel's sake. Teach us to communicate its truth joyfully to a lost and dying world around us, so that Christ will be worshiped, admired, and treasured for the great work he has done. We pray in Jesus' powerful name, amen.

✤ ASSURANCE OF PARDON: 1 JOHN 5:11–13

This is the testimony, that God gave us eternal life, and this life is in his Son. Whoever has the Son has life; whoever does not have the Son of God does not have life.

I write these things to you who believe in the name of the Son of God, that you may know that you have eternal life.

✤ HYMNS

"He Will Hold Me Fast"
"I Know Whom I Have Believed"
"Nothing That My Hands Can Do"

THE DIVINE JUDGE

✤ CALL TO CONFESSION: ROMANS 2:1–5

Therefore you have no excuse, O man, every one of you who judges. For in passing judgment on another you condemn yourself, because you, the judge, practice the very same things. We know that the judgment of God rightly falls on those who practice such things. Do you suppose, O man—you who judge those who practice such things and yet do them yourself—that you will escape the judgment of God? Or do you presume on the riches of his kindness and forbearance and patience, not knowing that God's kindness is meant to lead you to repentance? But because of your hard and impenitent heart you are storing up wrath for yourself on the day of wrath when God's righteous judgment will be revealed.

✤ PRAYER OF CONFESSION

Righteous Judge of all the earth,

We are grateful for your forgiveness and amazed that you would look on Christ and pardon us. We do not deserve your mercy, but we have tasted the sweetness of your love, and our hearts are full of joy. At one moment we can praise you that we are not condemned; yet with our next thought we freely judge and condemn others. We judge their appearance, their education, their spirituality, their wisdom and gifts, their knowledge of Scripture, their theological beliefs, their political opinions, their works of service, and their ability to love others well. We even judge others for things we do ourselves, slaughtering them in our hearts and rehearsing their weaknesses in our minds. With our mouths and thoughts we declare others worthless, using their weaknesses to feel superior to them. Father, forgive us.

Jesus, you were judged in our place. Though you had every right to judge us, you came not to condemn the world but to save lost sinners like us. You have been punished for all of our bitter, selfish, and prideful thoughts of judgment against others, and you replace our sinful record of hypocrisy with your own gracious perfection. Thank you.

Holy Spirit, help us to notice our judgmental thoughts. Reveal them to us, and draw us to repent and to run to you for help. Help us to love and forgive others as we have been loved and forgiven in Christ. Give us compassion and humility in order to discern rightly and leave judgment in your wise and loving hands. When we fail miserably, as we often do, help us to repent, confess, ask forgiveness, and rejoice that there is now no condemnation for those who are united to Christ. May that truth transform us and motivate us to live lives of kindness and gentleness with one another. Amen.

✤ ASSURANCE OF PARDON: HEBREWS 12:18–24

For you have not come to what may be touched, a blazing fire and darkness and gloom and a tempest and the sound of a trumpet and a voice whose words made the hearers beg that no further messages be spoken to them. For they could not endure the order that was given, "If even a beast touches the mountain, it shall be stoned." Indeed, so terrifying was the sight that Moses said, "I tremble with fear." But you have come to Mount Zion and to the city of the living God, the heavenly Jerusalem, and to innumerable angels in festal gathering, and to the assembly of the firstborn who are enrolled in heaven, and to God, the judge of all, and to the spirits of the righteous made perfect, and to Jesus, the mediator of a new covenant, and to the sprinkled blood that speaks a better word than the blood of Abel.

✤ HYMNS

"Before the Throne of God Above"
"Depth of Mercy"
"Jesus, Be My All (How Sad Our State)"

GOD'S KINDNESS

✤ CALL TO CONFESSION: ROMANS 2:4–5

Do you presume on the riches of his kindness and forbearance and patience, not knowing that God's kindness is meant to lead you to repentance? But because of your hard and impenitent heart you are storing up wrath for yourself on the day of wrath when God's righteous judgment will be revealed.

✤ PRAYER OF CONFESSION

Precious heavenly Father,

Your kindness to us in Christ overwhelms us. In him your justice is satisfied; you cover us with the perfect righteousness of your beloved Son. Every bitter thought we entertain, every evil deed we have done and still do, every harsh, unkind, and false word we have spoken and will speak in the future—all are completely replaced with the specific goodness and obedience of our Savior. Father, we thank you for such a great salvation. Your tender compassion toward us in our weakness melts our hearts with admiration, joy, and the courage to come to you.

Lord, we grieve that, in spite of your rich kindness to us, we still choose evil instead of obedience to you many times each day. You are the light—the giver of all light—yet we are prone to wander toward darkness in order to hide our sin and cherish our secret pleasures. You are the fountain of life, yet we kill others in our hearts with our selfishness and hate. Instead of fearing you with holy reverence, we fear what others think of us; we fear sickness, poverty, embarrassment, loneliness, or unbearable sorrow; we fear a life that doesn't go our way; and we fear that you won't give us what we crave. Almighty God, forgive us—prolong your kindness to us, and have mercy on us in our foolishness and sin.

Holy Spirit, captivate us with the love of our kind and righteous God. It is unthinkable that dirty, sinful people like us should be welcomed to find shelter, forgiveness, and love under the shadow of our great Creator's wings. We struggle to believe this is true, and Satan whispers that it cannot be. Persuade us of the truth of the gospel, and beckon us—draw us to hide away in the love of Christ, who has paid for all our sin and who covers us with his goodness every day. May we look to the future with hope and confidence—not in our ability to obey you, but in your unstoppable plan to rescue people like us. Help us to feast on your Word richly, to drink from the gushing fountain of your great love, and to eagerly seek to grow in holiness, humility, and dependence on you alone for our joy and salvation. In Jesus' name we pray, amen.

✤ ASSURANCE OF PARDON: PSALM 103:8–12

The LORD is merciful and gracious,
  slow to anger and abounding in steadfast love.
He will not always chide,
  nor will he keep his anger forever.
He does not deal with us according to our sins,
  nor repay us according to our iniquities.
For as high as the heavens are above the earth,
  so great is his steadfast love toward those who fear him;
as far as the east is from the west,
  so far does he remove our transgressions from us.

✤ HYMNS

"Hide Away in the Love of Jesus"
"I Will Glory in My Redeemer"
"Thy Mercy, My God"

JUSTICE (2)

❖ CALL TO CONFESSION: ROMANS 3:9–18

For we have already charged that all, both Jews and Greeks, are under sin, as it is written:

> "None is righteous, no, not one;
>   no one understands;
>   no one seeks for God.
> All have turned aside; together they have become worthless;
>   no one does good,
>   not even one."
> "Their throat is an open grave;
>   they use their tongues to deceive."
> "The venom of asps is under their lips."
>   "Their mouth is full of curses and bitterness."
> "Their feet are swift to shed blood;
>   in their paths are ruin and misery,
> and the way of peace they have not known."
>   "There is no fear of God before their eyes."

❖ PRAYER OF CONFESSION

God of justice and mercy,

We come before you as those who cannot endure your justice. If you were to keep a record of our sins, which of us could stand before you? Yet that has not stopped us from keeping a record of the sins of others, both real and imagined, and dredging it up against them repeatedly in the court of public opinion. We have dug a pit for others with our mouths, condemning them and justifying ourselves, often with scant regard to the truth of what really happened.

Moreover, when we ourselves are falsely condemned, we do not flee to your justice and plead with you to vindicate us. Instead, where we have been able to do so, we have fought back in our own power, repaying reviling with reviling, instead of returning good for evil. When we have no power to defend ourselves, we have sunk into depression and despair, bitterly angry with you for not protecting us in our time of need. Father, forgive us for our mistrust of your goodness.

Jesus, you could have righteously condemned people all around you. As the only one without sin, you could justly have cast the first stone. But instead, you deliberately chose to forgive those who assaulted you, whether with words or with blows. You spoke kind and gracious words to those who were sinking in their own sin, as well as just words of condemnation for the self-righteous. You committed your own cause into the hands of your Father, even as his face was turned away from you on the cross. On the third day, your trust in God's faithfulness was fully vindicated in your resurrection from the dead.

Holy Spirit, enable us to rest our case in your safe hands. Help us to trust you to take care of the earthly verdicts that others pass on us, in the light of the eternal verdict of "Not guilty!" that is ours in Christ. Help us not to malign others with our tongues, but instead to speak kind and uplifting words that combine truth and grace. Lift our eyes up to the heavenly tribunal, whose verdict on us has already been delivered, and so give us grateful, thankful, forgiven hearts. We pray in Jesus' merciful name, amen.

❖ ASSURANCE OF PARDON: PSALM 130:3–8

If you, O Lord, should mark iniquities,
    O Lord, who could stand?
But with you there is forgiveness,
    that you may be feared.

I wait for the Lord, my soul waits,
    and in his word I hope;
my soul waits for the Lord
    more than watchmen for the morning,
    more than watchmen for the morning.

O Israel, hope in the Lord!
    For with the Lord there is steadfast love,
    and with him is plentiful redemption.

And he will redeem Israel
from all his iniquities.

✤ HYMNS

"Alas! and Did My Savior Bleed?"
"Always Forgiven"

SACRIFICIAL SERVICE

✤ CALL TO CONFESSION: ROMANS 8:7–8

For the mind that is set on the flesh is hostile to God, for it does not submit to God's law; indeed, it cannot. Those who are in the flesh cannot please God.

✤ PRAYER OF CONFESSION

Heavenly Father,

As we consider the suffering of your Son in our place, we confess that we habitually look out for our own interests above those of others. Our homes and our churches are full of rivalry and conceit as we seek to advance ourselves and promote our own agendas. We do not submit our desires even to the desires of those whom we love most. We confess our relentless self-interest and pride, and we ask for your grace to change. Forgive us for desiring to rule others, for our daily failure to submit our lives to your will, and for failing to live with one another in an understanding way.

Lord Jesus, you were shattered so that we could be healed. Your life of selfless service to others, and your willing death in our place, give us all that we need to stand with confidence and joy before your holy Father. Thank you for being our faithful substitute in life and in death, and for putting yourself in harm's way for our eternal joy and safety. Thank you for submitting to your Father's will, even though you would have preferred not to drink from the cup of his wrath in our place.

Holy Spirit, we cannot lead the lives of sacrificial service to others to which we are called unless you change our hard and self-centered hearts. We desperately need your truth to convict us, your love to make us grateful for all you have done, your courage to compel us to submit ourselves willingly to one another, and your power to help us love others in their need. Have mercy on us, for we are weak and fearful. Transform us into humble servants who joyfully lay down our lives for one another in the name of our great and mighty King. Amen.

✠ ASSURANCE OF PARDON: GALATIANS 5:1; MATTHEW 11:28–30

For freedom Christ has set us free; stand firm therefore, and do not submit again to a yoke of slavery.

"Come to me, all who labor and are heavy laden, and I will give you rest. Take my yoke upon you, and learn from me, for I am gentle and lowly in heart, and you will find rest for your souls. For my yoke is easy, and my burden is light."

✠ HYMNS

"Thy Mercy, My God"
"When I Survey the Wondrous Cross"

TRUST

✤ CALL TO CONFESSION: ROMANS 8:16–18

The Spirit himself bears witness with our spirit that we are children of God, and if children, then heirs—heirs of God and fellow heirs with Christ, provided we suffer with him in order that we may also be glorified with him.

For I consider that the sufferings of this present time are not worth comparing with the glory that is to be revealed to us.

✤ PRAYER OF CONFESSION

Most high and glorious God,

We are full of toiling and fear, easily troubled and distressed, but you are forever at perfect peace. You are the same yesterday, today, and forever. You govern every atom in this universe with great care, working all things together for the good of your people and the glory of your great name. Father, we thank you, worship you, and proclaim that you are worthy of all our trust and loyalty.

We confess that we are easily distracted by the world around us. We know that you call us to suffer, and that our trials are meant to strengthen and train us, but our faith is weak and we hate to feel bad. We doubt and accuse you when we suffer pain, sorrow, injustice, rejection, loneliness, loss, disapproval, and failure. We are blinded by our emotions and prone to sinning in many ways in order to escape the painful feelings that overwhelm us and threaten to undo us. Father, forgive us for the sin that we embrace because we fail to trust that you are good, always for us, and never against us.

Thank you for the obedience of your precious Son, who counted it a joy to suffer great pain and sorrow for the glory of redeeming us. He trusted firmly in you and kept his mind and heart fixed on the prize that he cherished, which was his glory revealed in very weak and sinful people. Father, thank you for erasing our record of sin and doubt, and for replacing it with his record of spotless trust and of obedience through all his sufferings.

Holy Spirit, melt our cold, bitter, and fearful hearts with your great love for us. Take our eyes off of the earthly cities that dazzle us and that we are tempted to make our home. Instead, place our trust in the sure hope that we have an eternal home, a shining Savior who reigns in heaven and intercedes for us, a golden city that will make our present sufferings dim and unmemorable. Give us more grace to transfer our trust to the Savior who has suffered for us and will surely walk with us through the many valleys of death to which you may call us in our earthly lives. In our trials, draw us nearer to you, and shape us to look and think more like you. Teach us to count all things as trash compared to the great honor and deep joy of belonging to you, knowing that you will never forsake us or leave us alone. May the power of the resurrection be strongly at work within us, helping us to die to our strong feelings and to cast ourselves upon the mercy and love of the one who bled from his hands, his feet, and his side for our sake. We could never deserve such love, but we bow our hearts before you with humble gratitude and overwhelming joy. In Jesus' name we pray, amen.

✤ ASSURANCE OF PARDON: PHILIPPIANS 3:7–11

But whatever gain I had, I counted as loss for the sake of Christ. Indeed, I count everything as loss because of the surpassing worth of knowing Christ Jesus my Lord. For his sake I have suffered the loss of all things and count them as rubbish, in order that I may gain Christ and be found in him, not having a righteousness of my own that comes from the law, but that which comes through faith in Christ, the righteousness from God that depends on faith—that I may know him and the power of his resurrection, and may share his sufferings, becoming like him in his death, that by any means possible I may attain the resurrection from the dead.

✤ HYMNS

"Jesus Draw Me Ever Nearer"
"When I Survey the Wondrous Cross"

FINDING FAULT
WITH GOD

✤ CALL TO CONFESSION: ROMANS 9:14–24

What shall we say then? Is there injustice on God's part? By no means! For he says to Moses, "I will have mercy on whom I have mercy, and I will have compassion on whom I have compassion." So then it depends not on human will or exertion, but on God, who has mercy. For the Scripture says to Pharaoh, "For this very purpose I have raised you up, that I might show my power in you, and that my name might be proclaimed in all the earth." So then he has mercy on whomever he wills, and he hardens whomever he wills.

You will say to me then, "Why does he still find fault? For who can resist his will?" But who are you, O man, to answer back to God? Will what is molded say to its molder, "Why have you made me like this?" Has the potter no right over the clay, to make out of the same lump one vessel for honorable use and another for dishonorable use? What if God, desiring to show his wrath and to make known his power, has endured with much patience vessels of wrath prepared for destruction, in order to make known the riches of his glory for vessels of mercy, which he has prepared beforehand for glory—even us whom he has called, not from the Jews only but also from the Gentiles?

✤ PRAYER OF CONFESSION

Commander of the universe,

We marvel at your patient love for cosmic rebels like ourselves. We commit treason against you every day, with our lips and in our hearts. We grumble and complain as though you don't know our needs or care how we suffer. We argue with your providence, as though we are wiser and kinder than you are. We barge through life as though we are strong and can take care of ourselves and others. Our hearts flare with anger toward you when you don't answer our prayers as we wish, or do our bidding.

Father, forgive us for talking back to you. You would be just to destroy us instantly for our great sin. Instead, you have chosen to love us and to show us how patient and kind you are with foolish, weak, and bitter children. Father, thank you.

Holy Spirit, remind us often of the humility of Christ in our place. Though our hearts rise daily to accuse and condemn our Maker, he stood silent as a lamb and went to be slaughtered for our sin. He trusted himself to his Father in all things, without fear, grumbling, or complaining. When we talk back to God, show us our hearts and show us Christ. Though our sin weighs us down, his goodness lifts us up to heaven, where he stands today praying and interceding for us. Give us faith to believe that you are wiser and kinder than we could ever be. Give us the desire and strength to follow your commands, for without you we are nothing and can do nothing. We thank you that we cannot resist your will, and that you will always have your way with us in spite of all our sin. In our weakness, glorify our great Savior, whose love will never let us go, and whose death and shining obedience are enough to save all those who trust in him. Amen.

✦ ASSURANCE OF PARDON: ROMANS 9:25–26; JOHN 3:16–17

"Those who were not my people I will call 'my people,'
    and her who was not beloved I will call 'beloved.'"
"And in the very place where it was said to them, 'You are
    not my people,'
    there they will be called 'sons of the living God.'"

"For God so loved the world, that he gave his only Son, that whoever believes in him should not perish but have eternal life. For God did not send his Son into the world to condemn the world, but in order that the world might be saved through him."

✦ HYMNS

"Only Your Mercy"
"Thy Mercy, My God"

LIVING IN COMMUNITY

✦ CALL TO CONFESSION: ROMANS 14:13

Therefore let us not pass judgment on one another any longer, but rather decide never to put a stumbling block or hindrance in the way of a brother.

✦ PRAYER OF CONFESSION

Almighty God,

We come before you today to proclaim that you are excellent and that your glory is evident in all of creation. You are holy and perfect in all your ways, yet you stoop to love us, fallen and sinful rebels that we are. We do not deserve your kindness and care, yet you have set your love upon us. You pursue us with your everlasting promise to work all things for our good and your own glory. Father, melt our hearts with wonder, love, and praise to you.

We admit before you that we often find it difficult to live in community with one another, as you call us to. We are judgmental toward others, particularly when you have given us strength in an area where they are weak. We frequently struggle with malice, hypocrisy, envy, deceit, and slander. Though at times we may control our tongues, in our minds we rehearse endlessly the sins and weaknesses of others, as we try to justify ourselves and feel superior. At times we cause others to stumble into sin, and so do damage to their hearts and souls. Father, forgive us for the many sins that we commit each and every day. We cast ourselves on your mercy and thank you for the blood of Christ, which cleanses us from all sin, and for the obedience of Christ, which replaces our record of rebellion with the glory of his perfect holiness.

Holy Spirit of the living God, help us, we pray. Cause us to hunger for your Word and to grow in obedience to you. Help us to be faithful sojourners and joyful recipients of your grace.

Make Christ appear excellent to us and beautiful in our eyes as we worship, as we work, as we live together, and even when we sin against one another. Help us to recognize our sin and to repent quickly, asking forgiveness of one another and helping one another to find peace and joy in the goodness of your Son instead of in our own obedience. May your great and mighty power, which raised Christ from the dead, be strongly at work in each of us, helping us to love one another with powerful gratitude and to live lives of increasing holiness, purity, and love for you and for one another. In the excellent name of Jesus Christ we pray, amen.

✤ ASSURANCE OF PARDON: ROMANS 9:33; 1 CORINTHIANS 1:21–24

> Behold, I am laying in Zion a stone of stumbling, and a
> rock of offense;
> and whoever believes in him will not be put to shame.

For since, in the wisdom of God, the world did not know God through wisdom, it pleased God through the folly of what we preach to save those who believe. For Jews demand signs and Greeks seek wisdom, but we preach Christ crucified, a stumbling block to Jews and folly to Gentiles, but to those who are called, both Jews and Greeks, Christ the power of God and the wisdom of God.

✤ HYMNS

"Speak, O Lord"
"The Power of the Cross"

HOPE

✤ CALL TO CONFESSION: ROMANS 15:12–14

And again Isaiah says,

> "The root of Jesse will come,
>   even he who arises to rule the Gentiles;
> in him will the Gentiles hope."

May the God of hope fill you with all joy and peace in believing, so that by the power of the Holy Spirit you may abound in hope.

✤ PRAYER OF CONFESSION

Loving heavenly Father,

You alone are the Creator and Sustainer of all things. It is our great privilege to live under your omnipotence, righteousness, wisdom, mercy, and grace. You love us with better love than we could ever know here on earth, and we stand in awe of your power and your commitment to cherish us. Yet even though we have tasted your goodness, we are people who would rather trust in ourselves. We place our hope in our own talents and abilities, in relationships with people whom we admire and love, in our jobs and good health, in our economic value and academic abilities. We even place our hope in spiritual disciplines, thinking that we will merit more favor from you if we deny ourselves, pray constantly, or sacrifice for you and for others. Father, we are worshipers of ourselves, and find our hearts full of anxiety and depression when we discover that we cannot save ourselves in any way.

Jesus, if you had not lived a perfect life for us, we could never have hope or peace. You trusted your Father throughout your lifetime and into your undeserved death. Thank you for suffering the many agonies of life in a fallen world on our behalf, and for remaining faithful and obedient in temptation, grief, and loss. Your glowing obedience and perfect righteousness are the strong foundation for all our hope and peace. Though our faith and hope often burn low, and though we are full of weakness, your unshakable faith and hope shine brightly on our behalf and smother the gloomy darkness of our sinful nature. We marvel that you would consider us a joy worth suffering for, and we bow humbly before you and offer you our praise, our thanks, and our very lives.

Holy Spirit, teach us to be still and to know that you are God and we are not. Please give us godly sorrow for the many ways we sin against you, and fill us with repentance and hope in you. Open our blinded eyes to see clearly your faithfulness and power, your great love and unending patience, and your relentless determination to pursue us, captivate us, and ravish us with the truth of the gospel. Show us the unstoppable love of our Savior, who was stricken for our sin and who stands in heaven as our powerful advocate. Then we will be at peace, because you are perfect and strong and will never leave us, forsake us, or hurt us. Amen.

❖ ASSURANCE OF PARDON: EZEKIEL 36:25–29; GALATIANS 5:5

"I will sprinkle clean water on you, and you shall be clean from all your uncleannesses, and from all your idols I will cleanse you. And I will give you a new heart, and a new spirit I will put within you. And I will remove the heart of stone from your flesh and give you a heart of flesh. And I will put my Spirit within you, and cause you to walk in my statutes and be careful to obey my rules. You shall dwell in the land that I gave to your fathers, and you shall be my people, and I will be your God. And I will deliver you from all your uncleannesses."

For through the Spirit, by faith, we ourselves eagerly wait for the hope of righteousness.

❖ HYMNS

"Jesus, My Only Hope"
"None Other Lamb"

GOD'S GOOD GIFTS

✛ CALL TO CONFESSION: 2 CORINTHIANS 8:9

For you know the grace of our Lord Jesus Christ, that though he was rich, yet for your sake he became poor, so that you by his poverty might become rich.

✛ PRAYER OF CONFESSION

Almighty God,

You never change. From age to age you are faithful to your promises, and you love to pour out generous blessings on your children. Like a good earthly father, you enjoy giving good gifts to those you love, and we have so much to be thankful for. We know that we are safe in your love, because your kindness to us does not depend on our faithfulness to you. We praise you, Lord, because you raise up the poor and needy; and, as spiritually poor and needy people, we need your constant care and attention.

Father, we should be filled with gratitude to you every minute of every day. We owe you everything, so our lives should be devoted to acts of generosity to you, to your church, and your family. We ought to give the very best that we have of our gifts, time, and material possessions to you, with glad and joyful hearts. Yet we confess that we don't even come close to honoring you in this way, Lord. We are often stingy in our giving to you and resentful of the demands that church and people place on our time. We are generous to ourselves and to those whom we love or wish to impress, but we rob you frequently by not giving to you in proportion to our great debt. Father, forgive us.

Jesus, thank you for giving your life and yourself so generously for us. You lived each day in perfect gratitude to your Father, giving thanks for your daily bread and giving your mind, heart, soul, and strength to serving us. In the end, you even gave your body as a sacrificial offering on the cross. How can we repay such amazing love?

Holy Spirit, teach us to excel in the grace of giving. Help our hearts to overflow with generosity to others in response to the outpouring of grace that we have received. Make us quick to identify and meet the needs around us, whether they are the needs of our church or the needs of one another. And, when we have done all that we can do, help us not to take pride in our giving, but to recognize that it is only a small return for your great generosity to us in Christ. In Jesus' precious name, amen.

❖ ASSURANCE OF PARDON: EPHESIANS 2:4–10

But God, being rich in mercy, because of the great love with which he loved us, even when we were dead in our trespasses, made us alive together with Christ—by grace you have been saved—and raised us up with him and seated us with him in the heavenly places in Christ Jesus, so that in the coming ages he might show the immeasurable riches of his grace in kindness toward us in Christ Jesus. For by grace you have been saved through faith. And this is not your own doing; it is the gift of God, not a result of works, so that no one may boast. For we are his workmanship, created in Christ Jesus for good works, which God prepared beforehand, that we should walk in them.

❖ HYMNS

"The Son of God Came Down"
"Thou Who Wast Rich"

BOASTING

I will not boast, except of my weaknesses. . . . To keep me from becoming conceited because of the surpassing greatness of the revelations, a thorn was given me in the flesh, a messenger of Satan to harass me, to keep me from becoming conceited. Three times I pleaded with the Lord about this, that it should leave me. But he said to me, "My grace is sufficient for you, for my power is made perfect in weakness." Therefore I will boast all the more gladly of my weaknesses, so that the power of Christ may rest upon me.

✤ PRAYER OF CONFESSION

Mighty Father,

We confess before you the deep-seated pride that leads us to parade our strength and goodness before others, while at the same time hiding and denying our weakness and sin. We boast about our hard work and our achievements, our intellectual prowess and our self-control, and even about our spiritual disciplines, as if any of these virtues came from ourselves. We exalt ourselves over others, mocking their weaknesses and failures, behind their backs and to their faces. Yet anything good within us is entirely your gift; left to ourselves, we are profoundly weak and broken people who wander astray like sheep, moment by moment and day after day. Forgive us, Lord!

Jesus, thank you that you love us just as we are and are not ashamed to be called our Brother. You took on the weakness of a human body and entered our broken world in order to live the life that we could not live. You humbly saw the needs of people around you, and you loved them in all of their sin and brokenness, serving them with compassion and a pure heart. Thank you that your perfect obedience is now credited to us, even though we still have selfish, proud hearts.

Holy Spirit, we cannot deliver ourselves from our sinful

brokenness. Help us to look to Jesus for our righteousness and salvation—he alone is our hope and refuge. Transform us, by your mercy and grace, into thankful, humble, watchful children who are eager to serve you. Rescue us each day from the pit of our own self-sufficiency. May the words of our mouths and the thoughts of our hearts be acceptable to you, our Rock and our Redeemer, in times of sorrow and times of peace, until the day when our faith becomes sight and our souls are made whole. Amen.

✤ ASSURANCE OF PARDON: ROMANS 8:2–4

For the law of the Spirit of life has set you free in Christ Jesus from the law of sin and death. For God has done what the law, weakened by the flesh, could not do. By sending his own Son in the likeness of sinful flesh and for sin, he condemned sin in the flesh, in order that the righteous requirement of the law might be fulfilled in us, who walk not according to the flesh but according to the Spirit.

✤ HYMNS

"A Debtor to Mercy"
"Jesus Paid It All"

TRUSTING OURSELVES

❖ CALL TO CONFESSION: GALATIANS 3:1–3

O foolish Galatians! Who has bewitched you? It was before your eyes that Jesus Christ was publicly portrayed as crucified. Let me ask you only this: Did you receive the Spirit by works of the law or by hearing with faith? Are you so foolish? Having begun by the Spirit, are you now being perfected by the flesh?

❖ PRAYER OF CONFESSION

Gracious Father,

We are as foolish as the Galatians. After receiving from you grace upon grace, and acknowledging our dependence upon your Spirit, we find ourselves constantly returning to our own efforts to construct a goodness in which we may boast. Instead of depending wholly upon Christ, we trust in the rags of our own pretended righteousness. This is evident in the way in which we use every scrap of our own performance to raise ourselves above others, and in the delight we take in pointing out the weaknesses and sins of others. We trust in our good theology, our church attendance, our Bible studies, our witnessing—in anything and everything apart from Christ alone.

Jesus, friend of sinners, thank you for your faithful holiness and humility. Although you lived a perfect life, you never used your righteousness to put down or exclude other people. Instead, while graciously exposing the emptiness of their claims to righteousness, you constantly invited them to come to you for rest, for peace, for hope, for strength, and for salvation. Thank you that you were crucified for us, so that we might be crucified along with you, dying to the condemnation that was deserved by our sin in your death. Now we have received from you a righteousness that has nothing to do with our families, our churches, or our performance, but is a free gift of your ransoming grace. All we have is you, and you are all we need.

Holy Spirit, raise us to new life in Christ so that we may fight against sin with all of the energy that you give us. May Christ live in and through us in ways that are visible to all; may it be seen that any power that we have is a gift of God and not from ourselves. May his grace pour out of us in compassion and welcome for outsiders and outcasts whom you are drawing to yourself through faith. And may our hearts hunger more and more for the day when our dying will be complete, our heaven-bound race will be run, and we will rise to complete newness of life and will see you face to face. In Jesus' name we pray, amen.

⊕ ASSURANCE OF PARDON: COLOSSIANS 2:2-3

[I pray that your] hearts may be encouraged, being knit together in love, to reach all the riches of full assurance of understanding and the knowledge of God's mystery, which is Christ, in whom are hidden all the treasures of wisdom and knowledge.

⊕ HYMNS

"All I Have Is Christ"
"Wonderful, Merciful Savior"

RECONCILIATION

✤ **CALL TO CONFESSION: EPHESIANS 2:11–22; ROMANS 8:5–6**

Therefore remember that at one time you Gentiles . . . were . . . separated from Christ, alienated from the commonwealth of Israel and strangers to the covenants of promise, having no hope and without God in the world. But now in Christ Jesus you who once were far off have been brought near by the blood of Christ. For he himself is our peace, who has made us both one and has broken down in his flesh the dividing wall of hostility by abolishing the law of commandments expressed in ordinances, that he might create in himself one new man in place of the two, so making peace, and might reconcile us both to God in one body through the cross. . . . He came and preached peace to you who were far off and peace to those who were near. For through him we both have access in one Spirit to the Father. So then you are no longer strangers and aliens, but you are fellow citizens with the saints and members of the household of God, built on the foundation of the apostles and prophets, Christ Jesus himself being the cornerstone, in whom the whole structure, being joined together, grows into a holy temple in the Lord. In him you also are being built together into a dwelling place for God by the Spirit.

For those who live according to the flesh set their minds on the things of the flesh, but those who live according to the Spirit set their minds on the things of the Spirit. For to set the mind on the flesh is death, but to set the mind on the Spirit is life and peace.

✤ **PRAYER OF CONFESSION**

God of our salvation,

    You have rescued us with your strong and holy arms, and we bow before you with joyful gratitude. You have destroyed dividing walls of hostility between us by uniting us to Christ and in Christ, so that now we are one body and one holy people. Thank you for bringing us near, for forgiving our sins, and for sending your Son to be our peace. We confess to you that we cannot live according to your Spirit unless you strengthen us. In spite of our family ties to one another, we are prone to aim weapons against one another instead of joining together to fight our real enemy. Our strong desires cause us to fight and quarrel—we arm our minds with bitter thoughts, our lips with hateful words, and our feet with hostility that runs from reconciliation instead of moving toward others. We spend many hours each day pursuing what we want, even if it means hurting others in the process. Father, forgive us for our many sins.

Lord Jesus, you have saved us with your strong and mighty righteousness. Your confidence in your Father's wisdom and love caused you to love others well when you came to earth. You walked through life healing, counseling, loving, and making peace with your brothers and sisters. The Spirit brought you into a desert of temptation, where you suffered Satan's cunning attack and emerged victorious, because you knew that we would need your righteousness in place of our filthy rags. You were nailed to a cross, where you gave up your life so that we could have peace with your Father and his wrath against our sin could be fully satisfied. Jesus, thank you for being our peace and for showing us what true peace looks like.

Holy Spirit, deliver us from our love of self. Free us to serve others joyfully and to seek their peace instead of seeing them as rivals and enemies. Unite us in our love for Christ and in our desire to stand against Satan's schemes. When we fall, help us to forgive one another and to find joy at the foot of the cross together. When we stand tall and strong, let us celebrate your goodness and mercy, acknowledging that we remain needy comrades gathered around the cross. Set our minds on you, regardless of our own performance, and cause us to meditate often on the grace in which we stand firm and on the blood that justifies us. Help us to rejoice in the hope of the glory of God until we see Jesus face to face. Amen.

✣ ASSURANCE OF PARDON: ROMANS 5:1–2, 6–9

Therefore, since we have been justified by faith, we have peace with God through our Lord Jesus Christ. Through him we have also obtained access by faith into this grace in which we stand, and we rejoice in hope of the glory of God. . . .

For while we were still weak, at the right time Christ died for the ungodly. For one will scarcely die for a righteous person—though perhaps for a good person one would dare even to die—but God shows his love for us in that while we were still sinners, Christ died for us. Since, therefore, we have now been justified by his blood, much more shall we be saved by him from the wrath of God.

✣ HYMNS

"Jesus, Priceless Treasure"
"Not What My Hands Have Done"

HUMILITY

✤ CALL TO CONFESSION: PHILIPPIANS 2:5–8

Have this mind among yourselves, which is yours in Christ Jesus, who, though he was in the form of God, did not count equality with God a thing to be grasped, but emptied himself, by taking the form of a servant, being born in the likeness of men. And being found in human form, he humbled himself by becoming obedient to the point of death, even death on a cross.

✤ PRAYER OF CONFESSION

Loving heavenly Father,

Forgive us for our arrogant boastfulness and self-confidence. We are constantly seeking to build our own kingdoms, or to seek your kingdom in ways that lift us up, instead of submitting to your authority in everything. We easily believe that we know better than you and that our plans are wiser than yours, as if we were equal to you, the Creator of the universe, instead of being fallen, sinful creatures. We hate humbling ourselves and would far rather exalt ourselves, shouting our own glories from the rooftops. We want people to bow their knees to us and to do our every bidding, instead of submitting ourselves to you.

Precious Savior, as the Son of God incarnate, you possessed all authority over things in heaven and things upon earth, but you gave up that power to become a servant of others. Thank you for healing the sick and freeing those who were demon-possessed. Thank you for patiently bearing with your proud and deeply confused disciples. Thank you for your patience with us, for we too are often arrogant and confused. Thank you for your willingness to go even to the cross for us, scorning its shame.

Holy Spirit, thank you for raising Christ from the dead and exalting him to the right hand of the Father, restoring him to his rightful glory. Bow our knees before Jesus in adoring wonder and praise. Help us to learn how we may decrease so that he may increase. Teach us how to point people away from ourselves, and toward him, all the days of our lives. In his glorious name we pray, amen.

✤ ASSURANCE OF PARDON: JOHN 10:17–18; PHILIPPIANS 2:9–11

[Jesus said,] "For this reason the Father loves me, because I lay down my life that I may take it up again. No one takes it from me, but I lay it down of my own accord. I have authority to lay it down, and I have authority to take it up again. This charge I have received from my Father."

Therefore God has highly exalted him and bestowed on him the name that is above every name, so that at the name of Jesus every knee should bow, in heaven and on earth and under the earth, and every tongue confess that Jesus Christ is Lord, to the glory of God the Father.

✤ HYMNS

"His Be the Victor's Name"
"Jesus! What a Friend for Sinners!"

ASSURANCE

✤ CALL TO CONFESSION: COLOSSIANS 2:1–3, HEBREWS 6:10–12

For I want you to know how great a struggle I have for you and for those at Laodicea and for all who have not seen me face to face, that their hearts may be encouraged, being knit together in love, to reach all the riches of full assurance of understanding and the knowledge of God's mystery, which is Christ, in whom are hidden all the treasures of wisdom and knowledge.

For God is not unjust so as to overlook your work and the love that you have shown for his name in serving the saints, as you still do. And we desire each one of you to show the same earnestness to have the full assurance of hope until the end, so that you may not be sluggish, but imitators of those who through faith and patience inherit the promises.

✤ PRAYER OF CONFESSION

Heavenly Father,

We confess before you the weakness of our grip on you. In good times, we declare with assurance that in Jesus we have a sympathetic High Priest and that you will never leave us nor forsake us. Yet when trials and troubles come, we quickly feel abandoned and alone, convinced that you have forgotten us. Instead of drawing near to the throne of grace, full of confidence in your love for us, our hearts are consumed with frustration and fear. Instead of reveling in our assurance in Christ, we lash out at those closest to us in anger, or withdraw within ourselves to sulk and hide, running to the idols that promise us escape or immediate relief from our pain. We quickly forget that our advocate has ascended into heaven in triumph and intercedes for us there. Father, forgive us.

Jesus, thank you that you entered this world of suffering and temptation as our merciful and compassionate High Priest. You know what it is to be tired and overwhelmed; you know what it is to feel excruciating pain and weakness; you know what it is to be abandoned and betrayed. Thank you that you were faithful in all these things for us, always trusting your Father, always revering him and obeying him from your heart. Thank you that you are completely without sin, and that you sprinkle our distrusting and disobedient hearts with clean water, washing us with your perfect and spotless holiness. Thank you for the gentleness with which you receive us, and for not reproaching us for our constant weakness, doubt, and folly.

Holy Spirit, help us to cling to Christ. Show us more clearly our eternal High Priest and advocate above. Help us to ponder more deeply his love for us when we are tempted to doubt it, and to stir one another up to love and good deeds. Intercede for us in our weakness, taking our incoherent prayers and presenting them perfectly before the Father. Strengthen us in growing holiness as you continue in us the good work that you have already begun, so that on the last day we might receive what you have promised us in Christ, along with all of the saints. In Jesus' name, amen.

✤ ASSURANCE OF PARDON: HEBREWS 4:14–16

Since then we have a great high priest who has passed through the heavens, Jesus, the Son of God, let us hold fast our confession. For we do not have a high priest who is unable to sympathize with our weaknesses, but one who in every respect has been tempted as we are, yet without sin. Let us then with confidence draw near to the throne of grace, that we may receive mercy and find grace to help in time of need.

✤ HYMNS

"Depth of Mercy"
"Jesus, My Great High Priest"

GLORY

If then you have been raised with Christ, seek the things that are above, where Christ is, seated at the right hand of God. Set your minds on things that are above, not on things that are on earth. For you have died, and your life is hidden with Christ in God. When Christ who is your life appears, then you also will appear with him in glory.

✤ PRAYER OF CONFESSION

Glorious Father,

Thank you that you have united our lives to Christ so completely that his perfect life was reckoned as ours, and his death for sin was counted as our death. We have died and been buried with him, and in him we shall live forever! Thank you that when he appears in glory, we too shall bask in that reflected glory and share in the glorious inheritance that he earned.

We confess that our minds are all too often not set upon these glorious heavenly truths. Our thoughts would rather wallow in a very earthly gutter. Instead of delighting in Christ and finding our glory and rest in him, we delight in our sins and seek glory and rest from our idols. Our minds are often focused on food, sex, relationships, work, achievements, and even our own attempts at achieving goodness, rather than being fixed on the glory of Christ and the gospel. When we do become aware of the depth of our sin, we are cast down and flounder in the bog of despair, as if our own flawed righteousness were what saved us, instead of running swiftly to you to confess and repent and receive your forgiveness.

Holy Spirit, renew our minds by your sanctifying power. Transform our thinking so that our repeated sin drives us repeatedly to Christ. Change our vision so that our earthly trials and difficulties lead us to ponder the surpassing glories that wait for us in heaven. Open our eyes so that we see one another as magnificent new creatures in Christ, awesome construction projects that you will bring to completion on the day of Christ Jesus. Renew our minds so that we become increasingly confident that you will certainly finish that same work in us, according to your own plan and timetable. Amen.

✢ ASSURANCE OF PARDON: ROMANS 8:34–37

Who is to condemn? Christ Jesus is the one who died—more than that, who was raised—who is at the right hand of God, who indeed is interceding for us. Who shall separate us from the love of Christ? Shall tribulation, or distress, or persecution, or famine, or nakedness, or danger, or sword? As it is written,

> "For your sake we are being killed all the day long;
> we are regarded as sheep to be slaughtered."

No, in all these things we are more than conquerors through him who loved us.

✢ HYMNS

"Before the Throne of God Above"
"I'll Rest in Christ"

THE WORD OF GOD (1)

✤ CALL TO CONFESSION: COLOSSIANS
3:16–17

Let the word of Christ dwell in you richly, teaching and admonishing one another in all wisdom, singing psalms and hymns and spiritual songs, with thankfulness in your hearts to God. And whatever you do, in word or deed, do everything in the name of the Lord Jesus, giving thanks to God the Father through him.

✤ PRAYER OF CONFESSION

Sovereign God,

You are the God who speaks and acts—you spoke and created the universe; you spoke and redeemed your people out of Egypt; you spoke and commanded them to obey your wise and good laws, which would lead to their blessing and wholeness. But they and we have ignored, neglected, forgotten, and despised your Word. We have left our Bibles untouched, preferring to divert ourselves with work, games, television shows, and the internet. We have sought guidance from our friends and from the gurus of this age, instead of seeking truth from you. Even when we know perfectly well what your Word commands, we repeatedly give in to temptation in order to feed our desires and our lusts, or simply to make our lives easier. Sometimes we even despise the good news of the gospel that is splashed across every page of the Word, preferring to condemn and hate ourselves for our sins rather than confess them and receive your free forgiveness.

Jesus, you are the Father's final Word to this lost world. As the living Word, you were engaged in creation. As the Word appeared in flesh, you came down to this world to redeem us. You constantly loved and obeyed your Father's revelation of himself, delighting in the Scriptures and using them skillfully to refute Satan's temptations. Now you give us your perfect love for the Word as a free gift, covering our half-hearted and bored indifference with your passionate delight in the truth.

Holy Spirit, you have been tasked with leading us into all

truth and bringing to our remembrance the things about Jesus. Stir up our dull hearts and energize our apathetic spirits! Give us a fresh enthusiasm to search the Scriptures, eagerly prizing the wisdom that they contain and thrilling in every new insight into the gospel. Show us Jesus on every page; stir our souls with the sufferings of Christ and the glories that await us in heaven. Motivate us to strive with every fiber of our being toward holiness, while comforting us with constant reminders of the righteousness that is ours already in Christ and the assurance that you will complete the good work you have begun in us on the day of his appearing. We pray in Jesus' name, amen.

✠ ASSURANCE OF PARDON: 1 JOHN 1:1–3; HEBREWS 1:2–4; 12:22–24

That which was from the beginning, which we have heard, which we have seen with our eyes, which we looked upon and have touched with our hands, concerning the word of life—the life was made manifest, and we have seen it, and testify to it and proclaim to you the eternal life, which was with the Father and was made manifest to us—that which we have seen and heard we proclaim also to you, so that you too may have fellowship with us; and indeed our fellowship is with the Father and with his Son Jesus Christ.

In these last days [God] has spoken to us by his Son, whom he appointed the heir of all things, through whom also he created the world. He is the radiance of the glory of God and the exact imprint of his nature, and he upholds the universe by the word of his power. After making purification for sins, he sat down at the right hand of the Majesty on high, having become as much superior to angels as the name he has inherited is more excellent than theirs.

But you have come to Mount Zion and to the city of the living God, the heavenly Jerusalem, and to innumerable angels in festal gathering, and to the assembly of the firstborn who are enrolled in heaven, and to God, the judge of all, and to the spirits of the righteous made perfect, and to Jesus, the mediator of a new covenant, and to the sprinkled blood that speaks a better word than the blood of Abel.

✦ HYMNS

"Laden with Guilt and Full of Fears"
"The Son of God Came Down"

UNBELIEF

Therefore, as the Holy Spirit says,

> "Today, if you hear his voice,
> do not harden your hearts as in the rebellion,
>   on the day of testing in the wilderness,
> where your fathers put me to the test
>   and saw my works for forty years.
> Therefore I was provoked with that generation,
> and said, 'They always go astray in their heart;
>   they have not known my ways.'
> As I swore in my wrath,
>   'They shall not enter my rest.'"

Take care, brothers, lest there be in any of you an evil, unbelieving heart, leading you to fall away from the living God. But exhort one another every day, as long as it is called "today," that none of you may be hardened by the deceitfulness of sin.

❖ PRAYER OF CONFESSION

Holy God,

We confess that we are people with evil and unbelieving hearts, who do not naturally trust you. We are stubborn and rebellious, habitually unwilling to hear your loving, fatherly voice. We have repeatedly provoked you, despised your words, and even despised your incarnate Word, Jesus Christ, pursuing him to death. We have wandered along our own ways, rebelling against your loving plan or treating it as second best, when that plan involves pain or not getting what we want. We have pursued our desires for physical and emotional comfort, approval from others, health, wealth, success, or intimacy. We have relied on the perverseness of abusing food, drink, sexuality, or other people in order to bring us rest. We often do not take care of ourselves, or exhort one another, and we are easily hardened by the deceitfulness of sin. Help our unbelief, Lord!

Dear Jesus, what a specific, staggering, atoning love you have shown us in the midst of our weakness. On our behalf, you flawlessly believed your Father. You relied perfectly on his Spirit and were willing to obey every element of his plan for your life. Your love for us and your trust in your Father caused you to be silent before your false accusers, and to endure torturous punishment for sins you did not commit. The sins for which you were dying were ours, and we are eternally, deeply grateful for this inconceivable act of love. Because you took on our sin, we are now as white as snow before the judgment seat, washed in the cleansing, healing stream of the blood drawn from your veins.

Help us, our Father, to trust you in the midst of this earthly life. We grow weary, and our strength is small, as we fight against the sin in our hearts and in the hearts of others. Help us to find our all in all in no less than Jesus Christ himself. Cause us to live so that others would see that the strength to trust you could never come from us. Help us to sing salvation songs at the midnight of our sufferings. Awaken us to trust you in the midst of this prison of sinful flesh, and remind us that our freedom has fully and finally been bought by the precious blood of Jesus. Amen.

✠ ASSURANCE OF PARDON: EZEKIEL 36:25–28; ISAIAH 28:16

"I will sprinkle clean water on you, and you shall be clean from all your uncleanesses, and from all your idols I will cleanse you. And I will give you a new heart, and a new spirit I will put within you. And I will remove the heart of stone from your flesh and give you a heart of flesh. And I will put my Spirit within you, and cause you to walk in my statutes and be careful to obey my rules. You shall dwell in the land that I gave to your fathers, and you shall be my people, and I will be your God."

Therefore thus says the Lord God,
  "Behold, I am the one who has laid as a foundation in Zion,
    a stone, a tested stone,

a precious cornerstone, of a sure foundation:
'Whoever believes will not be in haste.'"

✤ HYMNS

"I Know Whom I Have Believed"
"You Are My All in All"

THE WORD OF GOD (2)

❖ CALL TO CONFESSION: HEBREWS 4:12–13

For the word of God is living and active, sharper than any two-edged sword, piercing to the division of soul and of spirit, of joints and of marrow, and discerning the thoughts and intentions of the heart. And no creature is hidden from his sight, but all are naked and exposed to the eyes of him to whom we must give account.

❖ PRAYER OF CONFESSION

Our God and Author of all life,

We confess our inattentiveness to your Word. Though we enjoy the benefits of the Bible's accessibility—its clear translation, abundant circulation, and unhindered distribution—we often leave it unread, unopened, untouched. When we do turn to your Word, many times we do so with mixed motives. We search for justification for our own behavior or seek grounds for criticizing others. We fail to join intellectual interest with personal humility. We salve our consciences by trusting in our faithful devotions rather than in Jesus' faithful devotion. Or we fear and tremble at the condemnations of your Word, missing its main purpose of pointing us to the atoning work of Jesus, the Word incarnate. Father, forgive us.

Jesus, though you are the Word of God himself, through whom all things were made, who dwelt with your Father in perfect glory, you became flesh and dwelt among us. Thank you for living in complete dependence upon your Father's word. You always did exactly what he told you. You were nourished by every word that comes from him, even when you were physically starved. You perfectly countered the devil's temptations, and his strategy of distorting God's Word, with the most profound and full understanding of its every word and letter. Thank you for enduring our well-deserved penalty for ignoring and distorting Scripture, so that we might enjoy the rewards of your perfect obedience to all that your Father has spoken.

Holy Spirit, thank you for inspiring those who wrote and recorded God's Word. We ask that you enlighten our eyes, that we may understand what has been written. Help us to find our only refuge in the Word incarnate. Bind us in union to Jesus, so that the piercing power of the Word may not strike us down, but rather separate our sin from us. Turn our eyes away from the false promises of this life, and fix our minds constantly on the glorious reward that is set before us because of Jesus' victory. In Jesus' name we ask, amen.

✤ ASSURANCE OF PARDON: REVELATION 1:12, 14–18

Then I turned to see the voice that was speaking to me. . . . The hairs of his head were white, like white wool, like snow. His eyes were like a flame of fire, his feet were like burnished bronze, refined in a furnace, and his voice was like the roar of many waters. In his right hand he held seven stars, from his mouth came a sharp two-edged sword, and his face was like the sun shining in full strength.

When I saw him, I fell at his feet as though dead. But he laid his right hand on me, saying, "Fear not, I am the first and the last, and the living one. I died, and behold I am alive forevermore, and I have the keys of Death and Hades."

✤ HYMNS

"How Firm a Foundation"
"Jesus, Be My All (How Sad Our State)"

FAITH

❖ CALL TO CONFESSION: HEBREWS 11:1–3;
   JUDE 20–25

Now faith is the assurance of things hoped for, the conviction of things not seen. For by it the people of old received their commendation. By faith we understand that the universe was created by the word of God, so that what is seen was not made out of things that are visible.

But you, beloved, building yourselves up in your most holy faith and praying in the Holy Spirit, keep yourselves in the love of God, waiting for the mercy of our Lord Jesus Christ that leads to eternal life. And have mercy on those who doubt; save others by snatching them out of the fire; to others show mercy with fear, hating even the garment stained by the flesh.

Now to him who is able to keep you from stumbling and to present you blameless before the presence of his glory with great joy, to the only God, our Savior, through Jesus Christ our Lord, be glory, majesty, dominion, and authority, before all time and now and forever. Amen.

❖ PRAYER OF CONFESSION

Commander of the universe,

You are powerful and majestic, and we marvel that you take notice of us. We, your creatures, have rebelled against your authority, yet you set your love on us and rescued us from death and hell. We praise you for choosing to pursue us and for giving us faith to believe in your Son.

Forgive us for believing that we are the captains of our own faith. Even as your redeemed people, we are easily confused and confounded. We deceive ourselves often and take credit for your good work in our lives. When our faith is strong, we think it is because of our obedience, devotion, and determination. When our faith is weak, we are frightened and full of despair, fearing that you have abandoned us because of our sin. Father, forgive us for not knowing and understanding you better. You are always for us, always working to grow us in your way and in your time. You have dealt with our sin once and for all, and in Christ we possess perfect faith and trust. Father, we are grateful that our sin cannot stop you from having your way with us.

Holy Spirit, the law of condemnation is written on our hearts and minds, and Satan easily enslaves us with it. Show us daily that your mercy is not purchased by our faithfulness, but has been bought for us by the obedience of Christ. Strengthen our faith according to your holy will, and help our rebellious souls to submit to you. Make us hungry for truth that will strengthen our wavering faith. Help us to bathe our minds in the good news of our oneness with Christ, and make that reality a strong and mighty shield that protects us in seasons of weak faith. Let us be grateful when faith is strong, for you alone are the giver and perfecter of faith. Let us not be shaken when our faith is weak and Satan terrifies our souls, for even Satan must obey you, and you hold us safely in your mighty arms. Help us not to despise ourselves and others when we struggle with doubt, but to lead each other patiently to the cross of Christ, who lifted the shield of his faith on our behalf and won our salvation and joy. In his strong name and for his glory we ask all these things, amen.

❖ ASSURANCE OF PARDON: HEBREWS 12:1–3

Therefore, since we are surrounded by so great a cloud of witnesses, let us also lay aside every weight, and sin which clings so closely, and let us run with endurance the race that is set before us, looking to Jesus, the founder and perfecter of our faith, who for the joy that was set before him endured the cross, despising the shame, and is seated at the right hand of the throne of God.

Consider him who endured from sinners such hostility against himself, so that you may not grow weary or fainthearted.

❖ HYMNS

"No, Not Despairingly"
"Rock of Ages"

GOD'S UNCHANGING FAITHFULNESS

❖ CALL TO CONFESSION: JAMES 1:5–8

If any of you lacks wisdom, let him ask God, who gives generously to all without reproach, and it will be given him. But let him ask in faith, with no doubting, for the one who doubts is like a wave of the sea that is driven and tossed by the wind. For that person must not suppose that he will receive anything from the Lord; he is a double-minded man, unstable in all his ways.

❖ PRAYER OF CONFESSION

Faithful and dependable Father,

We are unwise and fickle in all our ways. In Christ, we are new creations, full of noble desires to serve and obey you. In him we are full of faith and eager to delight you. But in our humanity, we are knitted to sinful flesh and double-minded in all our ways. Our motives are always mixed and tinged with selfishness and self-exaltation. We often doubt your love, your Word, your power, and your wisdom. We inherited our sinful nature from Adam, and we continue to choose to sin every day. Father, forgive us for this fallenness that will stick to us until the day we leave these sinful bodies behind. Thank you that in Christ you do not treat us as we deserve. Thank you for the hope that one day we will be only new creation and single-minded in our love and worship of you!

Lord Jesus, you never doubted the goodness of your Father or wandered from the mission that he gave to you. With single-minded faith and obedience, you suffered in our place. Though tempted and tried as we often are, you remained steadfastly the same, always devoted to rescuing inconsistent, faithless people like us. Thank you for your unchanging and unchangeable love and obedience that have become our own.

Holy Spirit, we desperately need your help in order to persevere and survive our own weakness and fickleness. Strengthen us with Christ. Give us the desire and ability to be steadfast and faithful in all our ways and to trust completely in our Savior. When you leave us to discover our wavering hearts, help us to acknowledge our foolishness and sin, and to hide in the ever-loving arms of Jesus. Help us to believe that his unchanging faithfulness is more than a match for all our unbelief and rebellion. Give us the gift of repentance, and replace our fear with wonder, love, and praise for our mighty Redeemer. In his unchanging name we pray, amen.

❖ ASSURANCE OF PARDON: JAMES 1:17; HEBREWS 13:8; MALACHI 3:6

Every good gift and every perfect gift is from above, coming down from the Father of lights, with whom there is no variation or shadow due to change.

❖❖❖

Jesus Christ is the same yesterday and today and forever.

❖❖❖

"For I the LORD do not change; therefore you, O children of Jacob, are not consumed."

❖ HYMNS

"Great Is Thy Faithfulness"
"Poor Sinner Dejected with Fear"

JUSTICE (3)

✦ CALL TO CONFESSION: JAMES 2:1-6, 8-9

Show no partiality as you hold the faith in our Lord Jesus Christ, the Lord of glory. For if a man wearing a gold ring and fine clothing comes into your assembly, and a poor man in shabby clothing also comes in, and if you pay attention to the one who wears the fine clothing and say, "You sit here in a good place," while you say to the poor man, "You stand over there," or, "Sit down at my feet," have you not then made distinctions among yourselves and become judges with evil thoughts? Listen, my beloved brothers, has not God chosen those who are poor in the world to be rich in faith and heirs of the kingdom, which he has promised to those who love him? But you have dishonored the poor man. . . .

If you really fulfill the royal law according to the Scripture, "You shall love your neighbor as yourself," you are doing well. But if you show partiality, you are committing sin and are convicted by the law as transgressors.

✦ PRAYER OF CONFESSION

Great rescuing God,

We are weak sinners who find it easy to move toward people who make us feel good about ourselves, comfortable, and important. We continually show favoritism in our hearts, and often with our words and actions. We hate others, sometimes for no good reason, and we do evil to them, damaging their reputations with gossip and rejoicing when bad things happen to them. We know we should love even those who do evil to us, but our sinful hearts rise up, and we seek "justice" by doing them damage in return. Some of us have hurt others by lashing out, while others exact vengeance by cold, deadly withdrawal. All of us have hated, gossiped, and slandered, rehearsing the downfall of our enemies with relish. Father, forgive us. Deliver us from ourselves; we are weary of our sinful depravity. Unless you rescue us, we live at the mercy of our own vindictive flesh.

Lord Jesus, we marvel at your faith. You did only good to others, yet the people you loved condemned you to death and mocked you as you died. They rejoiced in your downfall and committed the greatest evil against you, yet you still forgave them. You trusted your Father to deliver you, even when he turned his back on you. You did not retaliate, exact vengeance, or use your great power to deliver yourself. Jesus, we thank you for giving this shining obedience to us. We know that in this life we will never get close to your perfection; thank you for earning our salvation with your spotless record and for covering us with your obedience. Thank you for your priceless death that paid the debt.

Holy Spirit, help us to survive our weakness and our failure to trust you with our deliverance. Remind us often that all our sin is paid for—past, present, and future. May this truth give us courage to see our hearts clearly, to confess our sin readily, to repent quickly, and to try hard to love those who sin against us. Restrain our tongues and bodies, and keep us from trying to deliver ourselves. Give us patience to be imperfect, and to allow others to be imperfect, as we wait for your work in your time. Give us faith to trust that you are the holy Judge who will carry out perfect vengeance and perfect forgiveness according to your perfect will. Thank you that the day will come when we will see our glorious Redeemer face to face and be like him forever. Amen.

✤ ASSURANCE OF PARDON: COLOSSIANS 2:13–15

And you, who were dead in your trespasses and the uncircumcision of your flesh, God made alive together with him, having forgiven us all our trespasses, by canceling the record of debt that stood against us with its legal demands. This he set aside, nailing it to the cross. He disarmed the rulers and authorities and put them to open shame, by triumphing over them in him.

✤ HYMNS

"A Debtor to Mercy"
"Come Ye Sinners"
"I Will Glory in My Redeemer"

BEAUTY (2)

✤ CALL TO CONFESSION: 1 PETER 3:3–5

Do not let your adorning be external . . . but let your adorning be the hidden person of the heart with the imperishable beauty of a gentle and quiet spirit, which in God's sight is very precious.

✤ PRAYER OF CONFESSION

Loving heavenly Father,

You created a beautiful world, fashioning men and women in your glorious image to reflect your beauty and delight in your love. When Adam and Eve chose to sin, that image became marred and broken, and we confess that, like them, we choose to sin many times each day. We feel the ugliness of our fallen souls, and we try to make ourselves beautiful in many different ways. We love beautiful people, hoping that their beauty will make us feel more lovely. We compete with others in order to feel superior, and we crave the approval of important people in our lives. Some of us work very hard to make our bodies more attractive, in order to distract attention from our fallenness. Some of us are driven to academic, intellectual, artistic, and athletic excellence as we desperately seek to feel worthwhile. Father, forgive us for hiding from you in shame and for trying to weave robes of our own righteousness to cover our nakedness.

Lord Jesus, you left the glorious beauty of heaven to be born as a weak human being for us. You had no stately form or majesty to bring you honor on earth, but instead you clothed yourself in humility in order to invade our fallen world and rescue broken and ugly people like us. You cared for the sick, the weak, the poor, and the most insignificant members of society, blessedly focused on others and not on yourself. You loved with a gentle and quiet spirit, obeying your Father in every act of caring kindness. You became sin for us, taking on our twisted darkness and bearing the ugliness of the punishment that we deserve. You rose from the grave and gave us your obedience like a beautiful gift, shining and perfect in every way. Jesus, thank you.

Holy Spirit, make us beautiful in Christ. Help us to cherish the glory that we already have in our Savior until we feel no need to hide ourselves, to dress ourselves up, or to compete with one another. Persuade us that in Christ we are always captivatingly gorgeous to our Father, who looks on us and sees Jesus in our place. Grant us sweet conviction and repentance when we adorn ourselves with good works and beautiful things in order to feel better about ourselves. May the beauty of our Savior captivate us until we become more and more like him. Help us to love the unbeautiful and the unlovable with tender hearts that look beyond outward appearances to see people in need of forgiveness and love. Ravish us with your beautiful, unstoppable love until we see you face to face and are undone by your glory and perfection. In Jesus' strong and shining name we pray, amen.

✤ ASSURANCE OF PARDON: ISAIAH 62:2–4

The nations shall see your righteousness,
    and all the kings your glory,
and you shall be called by a new name
    that the mouth of the LORD will give.
You shall be a crown of beauty in the hand of the LORD,
    and a royal diadem in the hand of your God.
You shall no more be termed Forsaken,
    and your land shall no more be termed Desolate,
but you shall be called My Delight Is in Her,
. . . .
for the LORD delights in you.

✤ HYMNS

"Behold Our God"
"O Sacred Head, Now Wounded"

GOD'S GOODNESS

✦ CALL TO CONFESSION: 1 PETER 3:8–14

Finally, all of you, have unity of mind, sympathy, brotherly love, a tender heart, and a humble mind. Do not repay evil for evil or reviling for reviling, but on the contrary, bless, for to this you were called, that you may obtain a blessing. For

> "Whoever desires to love life
>   and see good days,
> let him keep his tongue from evil
>   and his lips from speaking deceit;
> let him turn away from evil and do good;
>   let him seek peace and pursue it.
> For the eyes of the Lord are on the righteous,
>   and his ears are open to their prayer.
> But the face of the Lord is against those who do evil."

Now who is there to harm you if you are zealous for what is good? But even if you should suffer for righteousness' sake, you will be blessed.

✦ PRAYER OF CONFESSION

King of love and mercy,
   How different would our lives be if we remembered that you are good and that you love to give good gifts to your children? Our sinful hearts are darkened and blind to the truth. In our weakness, we forget that you are good in every way and that you delight to fill our lives with all that is best for our eternal prosperity. When we feel guilty for our sin, we hide from you, thinking that you will judge us for our crimes. We forget that Christ has paid the penalty for all our sins—past, present, and future. When we feel sad, endangered, and threatened, we panic and turn to habitual salvation strategies that seem to bring relief. Fear makes us forget all your goodness to us in the past and tells us you don't care for the crushed and brokenhearted. Our idols

dazzle us with dreams of adulation, safety, prosperity, escape, comfort, and success, and we fall at their feet in worship many times each day. Father, forgive us for our treasonous betrayal. Thank you for your patience and unshakable love.

Precious Savior, you were punished for our crimes so that we could receive all the good things you earned through your perfect obedience. You forgave those who did evil against you, and you perfectly loved your Father even when he didn't rescue you from death. You trusted in his excellent goodness when you were fearfully threatened and your life was in danger. You did not try to save yourself, even though you could have. Jesus, thank you for your perseverance and for giving us your goodness as a priceless gift. Thank you that your Spirit is at work within us, transforming us into your beautiful image.

Holy Spirit, help us to remember the goodness of our Father. When you turn us over to our forgetfulness and sin, help us to see that our plans and our idols are not good at all. Teach us the emptiness and horror of our self-worship. Show us your unfailing goodness, until we are undone by your kindness and our unworthiness. Melt our stony, determined hearts with your undeserved love, until we fall at your feet with hearts full of love and wonder. May your shining goodness make us willing and able to turn away from evil more and more, and to do the good to which you call us. In Christ's name we pray, amen.

✣ ASSURANCE OF PARDON: HEBREWS 5:7–9; PHILIPPIANS 2:8–10

In the days of his flesh, Jesus offered up prayers and supplications, with loud cries and tears, to him who was able to save him from death, and he was heard because of his reverence. Although he was a son, he learned obedience through what he suffered. And being made perfect, he became the source of eternal salvation to all who obey him.

And being found in human form, he humbled himself by becoming obedient to the point of death, even death on a cross. Therefore God has highly exalted him and bestowed on him the name that is above every name, so that at the name of Jesus every knee should bow, in heaven and on earth and under the earth.

✤ HYMNS

"Amazing Grace (My Chains Are Gone)"
"The King of Love My Shepherd Is"

FIERY TRIALS

✣ CALL TO CONFESSION: 1 PETER 4:12–13

Beloved, do not be surprised at the fiery trial when it comes upon you to test you, as though something strange were happening to you. But rejoice insofar as you share Christ's sufferings, that you may also rejoice and be glad when his glory is revealed.

✣ PRAYER OF CONFESSION

Heavenly Father,

We live in a frightening world. In our fear, we often forget that you are powerful and loving and are devoted to your children. When we hear of wars and terrorists, we are tempted to turn to politicians to rescue us, and we panic despairingly if we feel we can't trust them. When faced with illness and mortality, we turn to doctors, diets, and frenetic health strategies in order to avoid the inevitable. When friendships fail and relationships disappoint us, we struggle with bitterness, anger, and depression because we have looked to other weak sinners to find comfort and meaning in life. When our plans don't work out, we scramble to construct self-salvation strategies in order to calm our fears and give us a measure of confidence and peace. Father, forgive us for forgetting that you love us, for stubbornly laying all our hopes and dreams at the feet of our idols, for despising you when you lovingly interfere with our self-salvation campaigns in order to rescue us from our pride and self-trust.

Thank you for your great patience with weak sinners like us, who refuse to turn to you until all else has failed. Thank you for bringing suffering into our lives and for letting our sinful hearts pour out of us, so that we can see our sin and repent before you. Thank you for causing our best plans to fail so we will learn that you are wiser, stronger, kinder, and more loving than we ever dreamed possible. Thank you for Christ, who faced fear and suffering with great dread, and yet turned to you in his moments of terror and temptation, trusting in your plan in spite of his horrible feelings. Thank you that his faithful determination to fix his eyes on you and to trust you in spite of the evil that he faced has now been credited to our account, and that you welcome us as perfect trusters. Thank you that you hold this world in your hand and promise that all will be well in the end. Thank you for the Holy Spirit, who lives in us and is at work every moment to help us grow, to comfort us, and to help us look away from our scary world and scary hearts so that we may see the beauty of our remarkable Savior.

Help us to remember your promises, to believe them, and to run to you in the midst of our fears with hearts that are bursting with gratitude and growing confidence in you alone. Amen.

✤ ASSURANCE OF PARDON: MARK 8:31; 10:45; 1 PETER 5:10–11

[Jesus] began to teach them that the Son of Man must suffer many things and be rejected by the elders and the chief priests and the scribes and be killed, and after three days rise again.

✤✤✤

"For . . . the Son of Man came not to be served but to serve, and to give his life as a ransom for many."

✤✤✤

After you have suffered a little while, the God of all grace, who has called you to his eternal glory in Christ, will himself restore, confirm, strengthen, and establish you. To him be the dominion forever and ever. Amen.

✤ HYMNS

"Jesus! What a Friend for Sinners!"
"O Great God"

SUFFERING

✤ CALL TO CONFESSION: 1 PETER 4:19

Therefore let those who suffer according to God's will entrust their souls to a faithful Creator while doing good.

✤ PRAYER OF CONFESSION

Loving Savior,

You left the place of highest honor to put on our fallen flesh and walk through our broken world as one of us. You did not live in a palace and command men. Instead, you were born in a stable and you served mankind. You were not adored and revered by those around you; you were mocked and scorned and were hated by your own people. In your worst moments of grief and pain, your dearest friends stood far away because they were afraid and repulsed by your agony. Yet even in your moments of deepest anguish, you did not turn away from the one true God or give up in despair. You trusted your Father as he turned his back on you, and with dignity, confidence, and tremendous strength you used your last breath to commit your spirit into his hands. Precious Savior, thank you for your perfect goodness to the very end.

Lord, we confess that we are not like you. We often feel abandoned, even though you promised you would never leave us or forsake us. When darkness and fear hide your face from our sight, we are quick to despair, to believe lies, and to turn to other gods that we think will soothe us for a moment. We commit our spirits to our idols, finding refuge in them instead of remaining true to you in our bleakest hours. When we feel undone by our strong emotions, we escape quickly into sins that offer us false comfort and hollow love. Jesus, forgive us for being weak, disloyal betrayers. Thank you for being faithful to the very end; we desperately need your perfect obedience to cover our shame and replace our long history of sin.

Holy Spirit, help us to commit our spirits into your hands and to trust the stories of our lives to you. Remind us that our times are in your hands, not in our own or in the hands of those who despise us. Help us to believe you are wiser, stronger, and more loving than we could ever dream, and to run to you for refuge. Help us not to despair when our idols fail and our friends abandon us. Instead, remind us of our Savior—of the feelings he felt and the sorrow he knew, of the pain he willingly walked into for us. Connect us to the heart of Jesus so that we might feel honored to suffer with him and to know a small taste of what he endured for us. Strengthen us to be like him, to turn only to him, and to rest in his perfect suffering. It is more than a match for our trembling souls. In Jesus' name, amen.

✤ ASSURANCE OF PARDON: LUKE 23:44–49

It was now about the sixth hour, and there was darkness over the whole land until the ninth hour, while the sun's light failed. And the curtain of the temple was torn in two. Then Jesus, calling out with a loud voice, said, "Father, into your hands I commit my spirit!" And having said this he breathed his last. Now when the centurion saw what had taken place, he praised God, saying, "Certainly this man was innocent!" And all the crowds that had assembled for this spectacle, when they saw what had taken place, returned home beating their breasts. And all his acquaintances and the women who had followed him from Galilee stood at a distance watching these things.

✤ HYMNS

"Dear Refuge of My Weary Soul"
"From the Depths of Woe"

WAITING (3)

✤ CALL TO CONFESSION: 2 PETER 3:9-14;
   PSALM 27:14

The Lord is not slow to fulfill his promise as some count slowness, but is patient toward you, not wishing that any should perish, but that all should reach repentance. But the day of the Lord will come like a thief, and then the heavens will pass away with a roar, and the heavenly bodies will be burned up and dissolved, and the earth and the works that are done on it will be exposed.

Since all these things are thus to be dissolved, what sort of people ought you to be in lives of holiness and godliness, waiting for and hastening the coming of the day of God. . . . According to his promise we are waiting for new heavens and a new earth in which righteousness dwells.

Therefore, beloved, since you are waiting for these, be diligent to be found by him without spot or blemish, and at peace.

✤✤✤

Wait for the LORD;
   be strong, and let your heart take courage;
   wait for the LORD!

✤ PRAYER OF CONFESSION

Sovereign Lord,

We confess before you our deep impatience and frustration with life in a fallen world. We strive and do not succeed; we pray and do not see answers; we ask for holiness and find ourselves seemingly stuck in our sin. As a result, we condemn you in our hearts and our words for your slowness to fulfil your promises. We easily become discouraged and give up the fight against our darling lusts. Where are you, Lord, when the struggle for holiness seems like a losing fight?

Teach us today that you treasure our humility more than our triumphs, our dependence more than our successes, and Christ's righteousness more than our best efforts. Teach us therefore to glory in our weakness, to boast in our inability, and to lift up Jesus as our only hope in life and death. Fix our longing eyes and hearts on your sure and certain promise that one day you will finish the good work you have begun in us and will present us to yourself utterly spotless. Remind us that your timetable for new creation is neither fast nor slow, but is in keeping with your perfect wisdom.

By your Spirit, Lord, help us to grasp the enormity of the new creation you have already begun in us. May that reality drive us to live lives of holiness and godliness as we wait, courageously straining every muscle and nerve in the ongoing war against sin. Teach us to long for the new heavens and the new earth, in which righteousness dwells, and to call others to share this glorious vision of hope. In the meantime, as we wait, grant us your peace in our hearts. Amen.

✣ ASSURANCE OF PARDON: ISAIAH 65:17–19; REVELATION 21:5–7

Behold, I create new heavens
  and a new earth,
and the former things shall not be remembered
  or come into mind.
But be glad and rejoice forever
  in that which I create;
for behold, I create Jerusalem to be a joy,
  and her people to be a gladness.
I will rejoice in Jerusalem
  and be glad in my people;
no more shall be heard in it the sound of weeping
  and the cry of distress.

✣✣✣

And he who was seated on the throne said, "Behold, I am making all things new." Also he said, "Write this down, for these words are trustworthy and true." And he said to me, "It is done! I am the Alpha and the Omega, the beginning and the end. To the thirsty I will give from the spring of the water of life without payment. The one who conquers will have this heritage, and I will be his God and he will be my son."

✠ HYMNS

"Out of the Depths"
"Revelation Song"

CONFESSING OUR SIN

✣ CALL TO CONFESSION: 1 JOHN 1:8–10

If we say we have no sin, we deceive ourselves, and the truth is not in us. If we confess our sins, he is faithful and just to forgive us our sins and to cleanse us from all unrighteousness. If we say we have not sinned, we make him a liar, and his word is not in us.

✣ PRAYER OF CONFESSION

O Lord, our holy God,

Help us and heal us. We are stubborn, blind people who repeatedly and willfully stray away from you. Like children who don't want their parents to hold their hands while walking through a dangerous city, we will not stay near you. In our blindness, even our ability to confess our sin has been distorted. Some of us are emotionally unaffected by the fact that we are helpless sinners without your mercy, and are indifferent to the cost of our rebellions. We speak words of confession out of principle, out of duty, and out of habit, but rarely out of awareness of our need and our helpless state. Others of us are so undone by our habitual falls into sin that we can barely look up to you for help. Lost in the anxiety of our unbelief, we speak words of confession out of fear, out of desperation, and out of hopelessness, but seldom out of confidence that you love us and have invited us into the blessedness of repentance and forgiveness.

Yet Christ has acknowledged our helpless estate and has shed his own blood for our souls. This blood gives us confidence to confess our failures to you. Where we have failed to approach you with honest, sincere, and confident words, Christ stands in our place, laying before you his heart in truth and passion, with no sin or mixed motives. As he hung on the cross, shredded for our iniquities, the sorrows that were rightfully ours were given to him in fullest measure. Your steadfast love surrounds us, because your steadfast love was taken away from him. What a precious, atoning, ransoming love!

Loving Father, create in us clean hearts that are truly broken for our remaining struggles with sin, yet are utterly confident that your love is more than enough to reach the foulest sinner who trusts in you. Give us this trust in great abundance, Lord, as we continue to wrestle through this earthly journey. Help us to sing now with confidence that Jesus truly is our only boast, and, when he returns to take his ransomed children home, let us sing anew, "Hallelujah, what a Savior!" In Jesus' name, amen.

✤ ASSURANCE OF PARDON: EPHESIANS 1:4–7

In love he predestined us for adoption to himself as sons through Jesus Christ, according to the purpose of his will, to the praise of his glorious grace, with which he has blessed us in the Beloved. In him we have redemption through his blood, the forgiveness of our trespasses, according to the riches of his grace.

✤ HYMNS

"All I Have Is Christ"
"All Must Be Well"
"It Is Well with My Soul"
"Man of Sorrows! What a Name"

WALKING
IN DARKNESS

✦ CALL TO CONFESSION: 1 JOHN 2:8–11

It is a new commandment that I am writing to you, which is true in him and in you, because the darkness is passing away and the true light is already shining. Whoever says he is in the light and hates his brother is still in darkness. Whoever loves his brother abides in the light, and in him there is no cause for stumbling. But whoever hates his brother is in the darkness and walks in the darkness, and does not know where he is going, because the darkness has blinded his eyes.

✦ PRAYER OF CONFESSION

God of light,

Our hearts are full of darkness, blinded by self-love. You have called us to love one another as you have loved us, but we confess before you our complete unwillingness and inability to obey this command. We are often consumed with jealousy and anger toward our brothers and sisters, hating them in our hearts. Instead of laying down our lives for others, we believe that they ought to serve us, and then we resent them when they fail to meet our expectations. Forgive us, Lord.

But amidst the darkness of our hearts we see a great Light. Lord Jesus, you are the Light of the World, come to make known your Father's grace and truth. When you left your throne to take on human flesh, you saw and loved people as they truly were, not for what you could get from them. Though tempted in every way as we are, you remained pure and undefiled, walking constantly in the light and loving us faithfully to the very end. Because of the darkness of our sin, your sinless body was hung bruised and bloodied on the cross. You set aside your glory, and entered the darkness of your Father's wrath that our sins had merited, for our salvation.

Lord, help us to walk as children of light who have been rescued from the grip of darkness. Help us to become people who want to obey because we know the light of your love. Draw us to meditate on the perfection of your Son, who never lifted his heart to an idol. Strengthen us to remember that his obedience and death have brought us to share in his glorious inheritance, and may this truth dissolve our hard hearts with gratitude. May we learn to walk in humble dependence on your truth day by day, trusting that your grace is sufficient for us to come boldly into your presence as cherished children. In Jesus' name, amen.

⬥ ASSURANCE OF PARDON: ISAIAH 9:2, 6; JOHN 1:4–5; 1 JOHN 2:7–8

The people who walked in darkness
    have seen a great light;
those who dwelt in a land of deep darkness,
    on them has light shone.
. . . .
For to us a child is born,
    to us a son is given;
and the government shall be upon his shoulder,
    and his name shall be called
Wonderful Counselor, Mighty God,
    Everlasting Father, Prince of Peace.

⬥⬥⬥

In [Jesus] was life, and the life was the light of men. The light shines in the darkness, and the darkness has not overcome it.

⬥⬥⬥

Beloved, I am writing you no new commandment, but an old commandment that you had from the beginning. . . . At the same time, it is a new commandment that I am writing to you, which is true in him and in you, because the darkness is passing away and the true light is already shining.

⬥ HYMNS

"Amazing Grace (My Chains Are Gone)"
"Who Is This?"

BEHOLD YOUR GOD!

✤ CALL TO CONFESSION: 1 JOHN 3:23–24

This is his commandment, that we believe in the name of his Son Jesus Christ and love one another, just as he has commanded us. Whoever keeps his commandments abides in God, and God in him. And by this we know that he abides in us, by the Spirit whom he has given us.

✤ PRAYER OF CONFESSION

Merciful and gracious God,

We come before you as people who desperately need to see you with clear vision. We need to behold your majesty in order to feel our smallness; we need to gaze upon your holiness in order to feel our sinfulness; we need to see your humble self-offering at the cross in order to know how truly loved we are. Father, as we contemplate your beauty, help us to see how unlike you we really are. We transgress your wise laws, love iniquity instead of righteousness, and sin freely against your holy character. Instead of believing in the name of Jesus Christ and loving one another, we trust in ourselves and our own efforts, while despising and mocking others for their weakness. Instead of forgiving others, we cast ourselves in the role of judge, eagerly repaying evil to those who have done evil to us. You, however, have shown steadfast love to us while we still hated you; you spoke words of forgiveness to us while we used your name as a curse; you have richly blessed us with the gift of your Spirit, even while we continue to look anywhere and everywhere else for our blessings.

Lord Jesus, you showed mercy and grace in the face of undeserved evil. You were mocked and beaten for us; when sinful men reviled you, you were silent like a sheep before its slaughterer; when people cursed you, instead of bringing deserved judgment upon them, you spoke words of forgiveness and blessing in return. Thank you for living the life of unmatched goodness toward God and your neighbor that we should have lived, and for taking our place under the curse that our sin merits.

Holy Spirit, help us to live lives that abide in Christ and are thus truly a blessing to those around us. Help us to love those who are unkind and unfair to us, to speak kind words to those who mock us, and to be gentle with those who are harsh. Thank you that your declaration of blessing upon us is sure and immovable, rooted and grounded in your unchanging and eternal character. Amen.

❖ ASSURANCE OF PARDON: ROMANS 10:9–10, 13

If you confess with your mouth that Jesus is Lord and believe in your heart that God raised him from the dead, you will be saved. For with the heart one believes and is justified, and with the mouth one confesses and is saved. . . . For "everyone who calls on the name of the Lord will be saved."

❖ HYMNS

"None Other Lamb"
"There Is a Redeemer"

GOD'S LOVE

✤ CALL TO CONFESSION: 1 JOHN 4:9–10

In this the love of God was made manifest among us, that God sent his only Son into the world, so that we might live through him. In this is love, not that we have loved God but that he loved us and sent his Son to be the propitiation for our sins.

✤ PRAYER OF CONFESSION

O heavenly Father,

Teach us to see that if Christ has pacified your wrath and satisfied your divine justice, he can also deliver us from our sins. Remind us often that you do not desire us, as justified sons and daughters, to live in self-confidence and rest on our own strength. You have given us the Spirit of life to live within us and to cause us to want to obey you; the Spirit and his power are ours because we are joined to Christ by faith.

Father, we are often confused by the sin that remains even though your Spirit dwells in us. We do not love others well, and we cannot come close to loving as we have been loved by you in Jesus. We are relentlessly selfish people who use others for our benefit and cannot love unconditionally. We are quick to anger, envy, covetousness, and sinful thoughts—even concerning the people we love the most. We make very small progress in holiness, and each new day seems to reveal more sin in us than we saw before. Help us to understand that the Spirit of life within us speaks to the law on our behalf and cancels the power of sin and death. We long to hear the words "You are good", but your Spirit whispers to us instead that Christ is good, and he will make us into his very likeness. We thank you, Holy Father, for giving your precious Son to die for our sin, and for crediting us with all of his glorious perfections, even as we continue to sin daily.

Holy Spirit, flood our souls with gratitude for the precious blood of Christ. When you strengthen us to obey, let us thank you for it and see your hand in it, lest we take credit for your work and grow proud. When we sin, humble us under our own depravity and make Christ beautiful to us. Give us grace to admit what is true about us, and grace to see what is true about Christ. Let us see our sin and treasure our Savior until we become brothers and sisters who forgive one another readily. Teach us to love one another freely, just as we have been cherished by our heavenly Father. May obedience to him be our greatest goal and highest honor, and gratitude our reason to strive for obedience time and time again. In the name and for the glory of Jesus Christ we pray, amen.

❖ ASSURANCE OF PARDON: JOHN 3:16–17

"For God so loved the world, that he gave his only Son, that whoever believes in him should not perish but have eternal life. For God did not send his Son into the world to condemn the world, but in order that the world might be saved through him."

❖ HYMNS

"Day by Day and with Each Passing Moment"
"How Deep the Father's Love"

LOVE ONE ANOTHER (2)

✦ CALL TO CONFESSION: 1 JOHN 4:11–13

Beloved, if God so loved us, we also ought to love one another. No one has ever seen God; if we love one another, God abides in us and his love is perfected in us.

By this we know that we abide in him and he in us, because he has given us of his Spirit.

✦ PRAYER OF CONFESSION

Loving heavenly Father,

We confess to you our inability to love and forgive others as we have been loved and forgiven in Christ. We are blinded by our own filthy righteousness and often find ourselves judging others for their sins in spite of our own lengthy record of transgression. We all hate people in our hearts, whether with icy cold resentment or red-hot fury, and we daily struggle to obey your command. Instead of laying down our lives, we murder the reputations of others with our bitter thoughts and spiteful words. Father, forgive us for our mountains of sin.

Lord Jesus, we are debtors to your mercy alone. Having received such vast forgiveness from you, we should love everyone freely and fully, and yet we cannot. How we thank you for loving your enemies, your disciples, and your closest friends and family with sinless perfection. You took on our failure and became sin so that we could be credited with your flawless record of love. You took the punishment for every evil thought we will ever have against others, for our aggressive sins of commission, and for our hateful sins of omission. How can we ever thank you for such a gift of love?

Holy Spirit of the living God, help us to repent daily of our resentments and evil thoughts, to confess our sins wisely to others, and to run to your throne of grace to plead for mercy and help in our many times of great need. Give us your wisdom to know when we should speak the truth in love to others, and when love can cover many sins, for we are easily confused. Make us sons and daughters who forgive with sincerity and with the desire to restore, so that we might reflect our glorious Savior as we struggle against this unforgiving, unloving flesh. We thank you that when we see you, we will love you and all of our brothers and sisters in Christ with perfect love, forever. Until then, keep us fighting against our sinful nature and striving to obey your commands. Keep us near the cross so that we will remember that all our failures are wiped away, and all our successes come from your loving hand. In the name of Jesus Christ we pray, amen.

✤ ASSURANCE OF PARDON: ROMANS 5:6–11

For while we were still weak, at the right time Christ died for the ungodly. For one will scarcely die for a righteous person—though perhaps for a good person one would dare even to die—but God shows his love for us in that while we were still sinners, Christ died for us. Since, therefore, we have now been justified by his blood, much more shall we be saved by him from the wrath of God. For if while we were enemies we were reconciled to God by the death of his Son, much more, now that we are reconciled, shall we be saved by his life. More than that, we also rejoice in God through our Lord Jesus Christ, through whom we have now received reconciliation.

✤ HYMNS

"Beneath the Cross of Jesus"
"Jesus, Keep Me Near the Cross"

INDEX OF THEMES

INDEX OF CALLS
TO CONFESSION

INDEX OF ASSURANCES OF PARDON

INDEX OF SERMON TEXTS FOR WHICH THE PRAYERS WERE WRITTEN

INDEX OF MUSICAL
RESOURCES

In our worship service, the prayer of confession and assurance of pardon are followed by hymns and songs related to their themes. Often the prayers of confession themselves allude to these songs, or to others used elsewhere in the service. The following is a list of the hymns and songs that we sing, keyed to particular prayers. Hymns are identified where possible with reference to the *Trinity Hymnal*, revised ed. (Suwanee, GA: Great Commission, 1990).

"Beneath the Cross of Jesus." Keith Getty and Kristyn Getty © 2005 Thankyou Music (EMI Christian Music Publishing). 65, 101, 237

"Be Thou My Vision" (*TH* 642). Eighth-century Irish; trans. Mary Byrne, 1905. 58

"Carried to the Table." L. Mooring, M. Byrd, and S. Hindalong © Blue Raft Music (EMI Christian Music Publishing). 46, 104

"Come, Thou Fount of Every Blessing" (*TH* 457). Robert Robinson, 1758. 38, 87, 122

"Come, Thou Long-Expected Jesus" (*TH* 196). Charles Wesley, 1744. 144

"Come Ye Sinners." Words: Joseph Hart, 1759; music: Matthew Smith © 2000 Detuned Radio Music (ASCAP). 46, 213

"Cornerstone." Words: Edward Mote, 1834; additional words and music: Eric Liljero, Jonas Myrin, and Reuben Morgan © 2011 Hillsong Music Publishing. 135

"Crown Him with Many Crowns" (*TH* 295). Matthew Bridges, 1851. 87

"Day by Day and with Each Passing Moment" (*TH* 676). Carolina Sandell Berg, 1865. 235

"Dear Refuge of My Weary Soul." Words: Anne Steel, 1716–1778; music: Kevin Twit © 1998 Kevin Twit Music (ASCAP). 223

"Debtor to Mercy, A." Words: Augustus Toplady, 1740–1778; music: Bob Kauflin © 1998 Sovereign Grace Music. 65, 159, 185, 213

"Depth of Mercy." Words: Charles Wesley, 1740; additional words and music: Bob Kauflin © 1998 Sovereign Grace Praise (BMI). 23, 165, 195

"From the Depths of Woe (Psalm 130)." Christopher Miner © 1997 Christopher Miner Music. 223

"God, Be Merciful to Me." Words: *The Psalter*, 1912; music: Christopher Miner © 1998 Christopher Miner Music. 16, 38, 58, 96, 129

"Great Is Thy Faithfulness" (*TH* 32). Thomas O. Chisholm, 1923. 90, 211

"Hark! the Herald Angels Sing" (*TH* 203). Charles Wesley, 1753. 148

"He Is Jesus." Stephen Altrogge © 2003 Sovereign Grace Praise (BMI). 141

"Here Is Love Vast as the Ocean." William Rees, 1876. 19

"He Was Wounded for Our Transgressions" (*TH* 244). Thomas O. Chisholm, 1941. 104

"He Will Hold Me Fast." Words: Ada Habershon, 1861–1918; alternate and additional words and music: Matthew Merker © 2013 Getty Music (BMI)/ Matthew Merker Music (BMI). 163

"Power of the Cross, The." Keith Getty and Stuart Townend © 2005 Thankyou Music (PRS). 179

"Revelation Song." Jennie Lee Riddle © 2004 Gateway Create Music. 141, 226
"Rock of Ages" (*TH* 500). Augustus Toplady, 1776. 209

"Servant King, The." Graham Kendrick © 1983 Thankyou Music. 153
"Son of God Came Down, The." Doug Plank © 2004 Sovereign Grace Worship (ASCAP). 126, 155, 183, 200
"Speak, O Lord." Keith Getty and Stuart Townend © 2005 Thankyou Music (PRS). 129, 179

"There Is a Redeemer." Melody Green © 1982 Birdwing Music (ASCAP)/Ears to Hear Music (ASCAP). 21, 233
"Thine Be the Glory" (*TH* 274). Edmond Budry, 1884. 34
"Thou Who Wast Rich" (*TH* 230). Frank Houghton, 1894–1972. 183
"Thy Mercy, My God." Words: John Stocker, 1776; music: Sandra McCracken © 2001 Same Old Dress Music (ASCAP). 115, 119, 167, 173, 177
"Turn Your Eyes upon Jesus" (*TH* 481). Helen H. Lemmel, 1922. 50

"When I Survey the Wondrous Cross" (*TH* 252). Isaac Watts, 1709. 41, 173, 175
"White as Snow." Leon Olguin © 1990 Maranatha! Music. 93
"Who Is This?" Words: W. W. How, 1867; music: Christopher Miner © 1998 Christopher Miner Music. 231
"Wonderful, Merciful Savior." Dawn Rogers and Eric Wyse © 1989 Word Music. 30, 99, 117, 187

"You Are My All in All." Dennis Jernigan © 1991 Shepherd's Heart Music (Dayspring Music). 82, 204

More Prayers of
Confession and Celebration

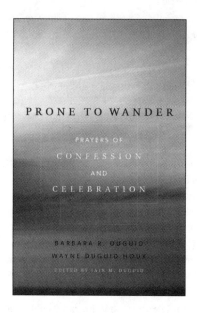

"This book calls us into the light, humbles us in our varied needs, delights us in God's many mercies. It is a resource for worshiping honestly and well. And it is a resource for living honestly and well."
  —**David Powlison**, executive director, Christian Counseling and Educational Foundation (CCEF), Glenside, Pennsylvania

"I find it easier to learn about God than to talk to him. These devotional prayers assist me in doing both, with the added benefit that they inspire me to pray those prayers with others."
  —**Edward T. Welch**, faculty member, CCEF, Glenside, Pennsylvania

"This book has many virtues. One is its flexibility in being adaptable to a range of situations, including public worship and private devotions. . . . I love its overall aims and method."
  —**Leland Ryken**, professor of English emeritus, Wheaton College, Wheaton, Illinois